CENTRAL PARK

A view of the Shelter, southwest corner of the Lake, 1869. From *A Description of the New York Central Park* by Clarence C. Cook.
New York Public Library.

CENTRAL PARK

A HISTORY AND A GUIDE

by Henry Hope Reed

CURATOR OF PARKS,
FORMER CURATOR OF CENTRAL PARK

and Sophia Duckworth

Clarkson N. Potter, Inc./Publisher **NEW YORK**

Distributed by Crown Publishers, Inc.

For
Jacob M. Kaplan
and
Alice M. Kaplan

hic tibi copia
manabit ad plenum benigno
ruris honorum opulenta cornu.
—Horace

Grateful acknowledgment is due to the following for permission to quote material in this book:

The Dial Press, Inc., for quotation from *Go Tell It on the Mountain* by James Baldwin. Copyright 1952, 1953 by James Baldwin. Dial edition, 1963.

The Macmillan Company, for quotation from *The Diary of George Templeton Strong*, edited by Allan Nevins and Milton Halsey Thomas. Copyright 1952 by The Macmillan Company.

G. P. Putnam's Sons, for quotation from *Memories of Samuel Parsons*, edited by Mabel Parsons. Copyright 1926 by G. P. Putnam's Sons.

Library of Congress Catalog Card Number: 66-22407
Printed in the United States of America
Design: Eugene Gordon

Revised Edition

ACKNOWLEDGMENTS

The authors wish to acknowledge the kind assistance of Albert K. Baragwanath and his staff at the Museum of the City of New York, Miss A. Rachel Minick of the New-York Historical Society, Mrs. John W. McNeely of the New York Junior League, Mrs. Alma C. Guillet, Professor John B. Patton of the University of Indiana, E. Powis Jones, Arturo Parrilla, Richard Edes Harrison, Elliott B. Nixon, David C. Mearns, Chief of Manuscript Division of the Library of Congress, Professor Albert Fein of Long Island University, Antoinette Kraushaar, Mrs. Martha McDowell, Pierce G. Rice and Bradford Green. Among the members of the Department of Parks they wish to thank Raymond J. Glespen (Public Relations), Gerhard Pollak and Charles J. Mulligan (Map Room), Daniel McPartlin, George Raimondi, Benjamin Cohen and Joseph Coticchio (Photography), Frank Sorace (Maintenance), Harry Krein (Recreation) and Peter Aschkenasy, Assistant to the Executive Director. Special thanks are due Clay Lancaster, Curator of Prospect Park; Walter Beretta, Curator of Monuments; Arthur F. Murphy in charge of planting, Division of Design; and Cornelius M. O'Shea, Horticulturist for the Borough of Manhattan, also of the department. Mrs. Charles F. Flynn kindly permitted the authors use of her extensive notes on Central Park history. And to the Museum of the City of New York, under whose kind auspices Henry Hope Reed conducted the two walking tours of the park.

CONTENTS

MAPS AND ILLUSTRATIONS

INTRODUCTION

A park is the most obvious ornament of a city. If that statement be questioned let anyone try to imagine a city without parks. What is more, they are the city's most popular ornament, the element of green in the urban fabric that appeals to all.

Among great urban parks the ones that stand out, the ones that are fixed in the public mind, are those at the city's center, easily reached by large numbers of citizens. It is enough to cite the Tuileries Garden in Paris, Hyde Park in London, and Central Park in New York. In many ways Central Park, as its name proclaims, is the most central. Other than the physical location there is its accessibility by mass public transportation; no less than nine subway stations are found along its borders, not to mention the numerous bus lines. More than location and accessibility, it is the visible factor, the encompassing wall of limestone, brick, and, lately, glass buildings, which underscores its centrality. The startling skyline seen from the park is a constant reminder that the great metropolis lies round about.

Despite the conspicuous site of Central Park it is astonishing how little of its history is known and how few have appreciated the amount of money and work, not to mention genius, behind its creation. Many otherwise well-informed persons believe that one day in the last century the city fenced off 840 rocky acres of Manhattan Island and declared them "park." American historians have been notorious in their neglect of Central Park as they have been of urban parks generally. Were the reader to peruse any standard high school or college text of American history, he must expect no mention of Central

Park as one of America's great works of art. If one of the park's designers, Frederick Law Olmsted, is noted, it is always as an observer, a traveler, or a correspondent of *The New York Times.* Historians often cite his vivid descriptions of the slave South of the 1850's, yet these same academic textbook writers never refer to him as our greatest landscape architect. The American historian's indifference to Olmsted, and, for that matter, to his partner Calvert Vaux, may disappear. The greater interest in environment and in the American city, as well as the fact that this year, 1972, is the sesquicentennial of Olmsted's birth, will probably set matters right in our history books.

In 1966, to overcome the too casual acceptance of the park, the city administration named one of the authors of this book Curator of Central Park, with the injunction to produce this book. In addition, in recognition of the park's importance, the Curator was to advise on how the park could be restored in keeping with the aims of its designers, Frederick Law Olmsted and Calvert Vaux.

It occurred to the Curator that the first step in that direction would be to eliminate cars from the park. A friend of his, Irvin J. Schwartz, suggested the wisest move would be to bar traffic on weekends and holidays as a starter. Their aim was to bring peace to the park as well as air unpolluted by car exhaust. The proposal was accepted and went into effect in the spring of 1966.

Closing Central Park and subsequently other city parks to traffic was hailed by an enthusiastic public as the most progressive measure of park policy in decades. Mr. Schwartz and the Curator took justifiable pride in their contribution because the public responded so wholeheartedly and because the measure cost the city nothing.

One quite unexpected result of the closing, at least for its two initiators, was the rediscovery of the park by cyclists. A renaissance of the bicycle has followed to the point where cycling in Central Park is part of a New York weekend.

Besides reducing noise and pollution, the barring of traffic held out the promise of a new respect and a new policy for the park, as did the creation of the curatorship. Instead, quite the opposite took place. Another kind of noise and pollution appeared in the form of strident commercial and political exploitation. Although it has receded somewhat, the exploitation remains. Central Park continues to be chosen by promoters, theatrical producers, and others because, as a site, it is unequaled for generating publicity.

As the reader will discover from the park's history, such invasion of the park is hardly new. Ever since its opening in October 1858, it has been subjected to constant pressure by special interests. Most of these groups proposed building some kind of special facility in the park. (On pages 42 and 43 a map shows those proposed only since 1900.) In the last century a minuscule number of structures did find their way in, the most important and largest being the Metropolitan Museum of Art. That both Olmsted and Vaux were aware of the possible threat posed by such invasions can be seen at Brooklyn's Prospect Park, which they also designed; there the borough of Brooklyn, on their advice, retained acreage *outside* the park for institutional use.

Had the Metropolitan Museum remained the only major invader it would have been another story, but it proved the first of many, all of which have occurred in this century. Most of them are, in themselves, valid; the tragic error was placing them in the park.

One invasion has been allowing patriotic, then religious, and finally political meetings and rallies to assemble in the park. Their presence must be put down to the failure of the city planners; even today those in charge of city planning have been incapable of providing public squares for civic ceremonies, meetings, and rallies. New York is conspicuous among world cities in not having monumental squares even for public ceremonies.

Another example of damaging park policy in recent years is the installation of a restaurant café at the Terrace on the Lake (see page 92). Eating *al fresco* is always pleasant in beautiful surroundings, but it is only possible under very special conditions; otherwise, the setting is destroyed. That is exactly what has occurred. An attempt to have a snack bar there in the 1930's and 1940's ended by damaging the soft Nova Scotia sandstone and irreplaceable Minton tile of the structure. The latest concessionaire has brought kitchen equipment, lockers, and garbage cans, as well as food kiosks, to the site. Other than ensuring the stink of garbage on hot weekends, the restaurant has destroyed one of the park's beautiful views, that of the Bethesda Fountain and the Lake seen through an arcade. Additional vandalism occurred when the concessionaire painted a portion of the sandstone a dirty pinkish grey. The paint has entered the soft stone and it is questionable if it can ever be removed without leaving scars. More damage is bound to follow unless the concession is canceled and the equipment and kiosks removed.

Another intrusion has been the introduction of nightlighting at the west end of the North Meadow on the latitude of 98th Street. Eight giant poles support eight batteries of blinding spotlights for night baseball. The facility never serves more than seventy-five persons, consisting of two teams and a small public. The glare from the spotlight is by no means confined to the park and has proven an objectionable nuisance to residents on both Central Park West and Fifth Avenue.

The indifference to park invasion and to pollution in fact, although those responsible have attacked pollution in theory, made easier the demands of the Metropolitan Museum of Art to expand. The museum expansion has an ironic touch. The institution is dedicated to art; for that reason it is allowed to help destroy one of America's greatest works of art—Central Park.

For well over a decade now the emphasis has been on more and more structures and statues in the park, accompanied by much talk of art and culture. Events in quantity are scheduled in the park, and publicity continues to focus on it. The supine retreat before exploiters might be condoned were the retreat matched by adequate maintenance. Quite the contrary has occurred—the maintenance is worse than it has ever been. In 1960 there were 115 laborers in the park; there were 74 in 1971. Presently there are only four gardeners. The increasing crowds have been welcomed by a melancholy spectacle of downtrodden shrubbery, dustbowl lawns, erosion, trash, and bridges—especially Bow Bridge on the Lake—neglected to the point of endangering the public. Indeed the oldest building in the park that was part of the original design, the Ball Players House, was destroyed in 1968 by indifference. And as the Belvedere Castle and its terrace continue to slip toward total ruin, they too will disappear.

The park's sad condition has been matched, unfortunately, by a total breakdown in public discipline. Poor maintenance has only encouraged a careless public attitude. Even city employees think nothing of parking their cars at the Wollman Skating Rink and at the south gatehouse of the Reservoir, converting lawn into a morass or a dustbowl.

Now the assumption of those responsible is that there is no other solution, yet a flow of news releases conveys messages of preservation, ecology, the importance of nature, and the need for more art and culture in the city. If the responsible persist in their defeatism—is there another word?—they are deceiving the public, for an answer lies in a positive, progressive policy. Such a policy would affirm that Central Park is a historic work of art ranking with the Statue of Liberty, the National Capitol,

Independence Hall, and "Washington Crossing the Delaware." As such it demands an end to invasions and pollution, including events better staged elsewhere. It would restrict picnicking, limit the number of vendors and their wagons—or keep them out altogether, for each one is a perambulating pigsty—and bar loud musical events, as their sound is simply another form of pollution. One day, perhaps, transistor radios without earplugs could well be outlawed in the park.

Such a policy would include desperately needed maintenance. The park must have an ample permanent staff of gardeners and laborers whose sole duty would be caring for the park. At present there are only two high maintenance areas, namely, the Zoo and the Arsenal at the south end and the Conservatory Garden at the north end. Others must be developed. The Ramble might be one. Another would be that section of the park south of the 65th Street transverse road. The latter is most frequented by tourists and other visitors, and it should reflect something of the pride New Yorkers have in their city. Of course, it will take special effort; where ground cover, flowering shrubs, and flowers are concerned, the work has to be executed with discretion and skill within the concept of a natural park. It would also mean that the public must be asked to respect the special attention by picnicking only in designated areas, by keeping dogs on leash, and by other signs of respect. Good maintenance has to be backed by a disciplined public. Without public manners in a park all the maintenance in the world will not save it from being a visual disaster.

Perhaps the federal government should intervene to furnish the needed spark in the park's maintenance. In 1965 the National Park Service of the Department of the Interior designated Central Park a National Historic Landmark (see page 52). Seeing that the city has failed to protect one of its great works of art, the park should be delisted and not designated again until the city has taken special measures, legal and financial, to protect it.

In the face of the persisting threats and persisting neglect, it is little short of a miracle that civic organizations and citizen groups have succeeded in taking certain positive steps for the park's improvement. Many organizations have had a role in defending the park and broadening the public's awareness of its importance. Among them are the Parks Council, the Save the Central Park Committee, the Sierra Club, the National Audubon Society, the New York Horticultural Society, the Linnaean Society, the Municipal Art Society, and the American Society of Landscape Architects. The most active body is the Friends of Central Park (Post Office Box 610, Lenox Hill Station, New York, N.Y. 10021), an entirely voluntary organization, it might be added. It distributes the popular map of the park, tree maps prepared with the cooperation of the Department's Forestry Division, and *Tree Trails in Central Park*. It launched the campaign to save the Ladies Pavilion on the west side of the Lake; the pavilion is being fully rebuilt by the Park Department. It has helped finance a tree surgery program. Like its sister organization in Brooklyn, Friends of Prospect Park, it sponsors walks, bicycle tours, and lectures throughout the year.

What is heartening about the renewed public interest in the park as a park—and not as a stage for commercial promotion nor as "Central Park Memorial Cemetery" for wealthy individuals bent on financing memorials to themselves—has been the response of the employees of the Park Department who, offered the opportunity, will give Central Park the attention it deserves. Department carpenters rebuilt the rustic shelters at the Lake landings—shelters allowed to disappear over the last thirty years. Instead of replacing a vandalized bridge in the Ramble with a concrete slab, the same carpenters built a rustic bridge of wood. The Department horticulturist, responding to the renewed interest, has planted a persimmon tree, Himalayan pines, and even a Camperdown elm, along with other species long absent from the park. And there are those who have pushed the program for removing obsolete asphalt areas and who are striving to have little-used access drives removed from circulation with the eventual aim of closing the park to cars altogether.

Modest efforts they may well be, but they represent the future. The promise held out by closing the park to traffic has not been lost altogether. A fresh appreciation of the park has revived the values of Frederick Law Olmsted and Calvert Vaux. These permanent values, too long forgotten, will be recognized again as the battle against pollution in all its forms —trash, noise, personal memorials, polluted air, and vandalism —continues to gain momentum.

Above and beyond the triumph over the forces of destruction will come the recognition of Central Park as one of the chief adornments of New York City.

HENRY HOPE REED
Curator of Parks
New York City

CENTRAL PARK

I

A HISTORY

Of all the city's wonders, Central Park ranks first in the affection of New Yorkers. Hundreds of thousands think of it as "their park." Twelve million wander through it yearly, making it the most heavily frequented park of its size in the world. The park is many things to many people. To the 840 acres set aside for public use right in the middle of the city come adults and children to ride horseback and bicycle, listen to concerts, play football, baseball, soccer, croquet, tennis and hockey, see Shakespearean plays, pitch horseshoes, sketch and paint, walk the dog, ride in horse-drawn carriages, dance, play chess and checkers, work out for track, romp in playgrounds, make movies and high-fashion shots, sail model boats, picnic, ice-skate, row on the lakes, see the marionette troupe, bowl on the greens, identify planting, visit the Zoo, wade in wading pools, bird-watch, go courting, or indulge in such activities as training for guerrilla warfare, as did some exiled Cubans not so long ago. Of course, many people come to the park to do none of these things; they come to relax and enjoy the free show the park itself always offers of nature's changing spectacle—the delicate blanket of a winter snow, the blossoms in May of the mock orange, azalea, hawthorn and wisteria or autumn's blaze when the leaves turn saffron and scarlet.

Poets, songwriters and composers have celebrated the delights of this park as no other, in verse, song and music. Few may know the "Central Park March" of the 1860's, but many remember *Up in Central Park*, a musical comedy of the 1940's.

Sociologists and city planners pay their respects to the park by referring to it as "the lungs of the city," without which New York might strangle. Central Park deserves fame and celebration, for it was the first and most influential of American landscaped parks; and it initiated the park and recreation movement in this country. Even now, in communities seeking to put aside land for future public use, it is cited as the great example of foresight in park planning. In 1965 the United States Government declared the park a National Historic Landmark.

Central Park was designed in 1858 by Frederick Law Olmsted and Calvert Vaux; it is wholly man-made. What seems nature's gift is the result of work and dreams. "Every foot of the park's surface, every tree and bush, as well as every arch, roadway and walk," wrote Olmsted, "has been fixed where it is with a *purpose*." In its design it represents a high degree of sophistication, the culmination of England's picturesque landscape tradition molded to American vision. If the Lower or Southern Section presents the pastoral of this tradition, the Upper or Northern Section presents the strictly picturesque or natural. Together they form a grand design, a closely knit unit where lawn, glade, water and wilderness weave in and out to push back the turbulent metropolis. Central Park is, in fact, a giant public garden, a supreme American work of art.

To understand how New York's park came to be and to appreciate the design selected it is necessary to know something of the American response to nature and, equally important, the story of landscape architecture. From the beginning Americans have, on the one hand, accepted land as so much real estate to be bought and sold and, on the other, they have professed admiration and even love for the country's natural wonders. There is the ever-present drive to exploit the countryside, and yet America the Beautiful is seen, first of all, in terms of nature's bounty. The New Yorker surrendered the harbor, a natural wonder, to wholesale exploitation and divided every foot of Manhattan Island into lots. The Commissioners Plan of 1811 spread the grid over the island, including Central Park, leaving only a few squares. James Fenimore Cooper found the city tiresome in the 1830's, because conversation at the dinner-table was limited to "*lots*."

In those days the New Yorker, eager for modest rural pleasures, sought out the Elysian Fields, part of the Stevens estate in Hoboken, on the other side of the Hudson, opposite 14th Street. But obviously the happily-named resort alone would not do for the growing city. New York had become the nation's gateway, and not a few of the new arrivals stopped at the gate instead of hurrying West. In 1820 the population was close to 124,000; by 1840 it was over 312,000. Four years later the poet William Cullen Bryant made one of the first demands for a park. "Commerce is devouring inch by inch the coast of the island," he warned in 1844, "and if we would rescue any part of it for health and recreation it must be done now. . . . All large cities have their extensive public grounds and gardens, Madrid and Mexico [City] their Alamedas, London its Regent's Park, Paris its Champs Elysées and Vienna its Prater." A year later he wrote in a letter that

> *the population of your city, increasing with such prodigious rapidity, your sultry summers, and corrupt atmosphere generated in hot and crowded streets, make it a cause of regret that in laying out New York, no preparation was made, while it was yet practicable, for a range of parks and public gardens along the central part of the island or elsewhere, to remain perpetually for the refreshment and recreation of the citizens during the torrid heats of the warm season. There are yet unoccupied lands on the island which might, I suppose, be procured for the purpose, and which, on account of their rocky and uneven surfaces, might be laid out into surpassingly beautiful pleasure-grounds, but, while we are discussing the subject, the advancing population of the city is sweeping over them and covering them from our reach.*

A second and equally powerful voice raised for a park was that of the landscape architect, Andrew Jackson Downing. "A large public park . . ." he wrote in 1849 in his magazine, *The Horticulturist*, "would not only *pay* in money, but largely civilize and refine the national character, foster the love of rural beauty, and increase the knowledge of, and taste for, rare and beautiful trees and plants. . . . The true policy of republics is to foster the taste for great public libraries, parks and gardens which *all* may enjoy."

Manhattan's "rocky and uneven surfaces" were not obstacles to Bryant, for they could and would be made "into surpassing and beautiful pleasure-gounds," which Downing saw as necessary to encourage the people's appreciation of "rural beauty." The demands of the two men, voiced on these shores for the first time, reflected an American current of a larger stream, the Romantic Movement, which saw in nature a refuge from the spreading Industrial Revolution. Even before Bryant and Downing spoke up, James Fenimore Cooper was writing some of the finest passages on the native wilderness. The descendants of men who had looked on nature as an enemy were turning away from the scarred landscape. While mourning what had been destroyed by greed and haste, they were discovering that American nature could be a vast garden.

Nature as a garden—the vision is as old as time. The Garden of Eden of the ancient Hebrews was founded on the tree-park of the Assyrians, and the word *paradise*, stems from the Persian word for a gardenlike park. If the people of Israel had but small gardens in their stony land, they loved flowers, whose names brighten the Song of Solomon. An early evocation of the pastoral landscape, the countryside beyond the garden, can be found in Hebrew poetry. "The Lord is my shepherd; I shall not want," run the opening lines of the 23rd Psalm. "He maketh me to lie down in green pastures: He leadeth me beside the still waters." Babylon is remembered for its hanging gardens, one of the seven wonders of the ancient world. The Greeks of the age of Pericles may not have known of gardens, but the Hellenistic Greeks took their cue from the Persians. Then, too, there was the tradition of pastoral poetry stemming from Theocritus, with its idealization of the bucolic life. The Romans, heirs to Alexander and Hellenism, had large gardens as part of their country and seaside villas. Virgil, following Theocritus, took the countryside as province, praising the rural life, *res rustica*, and especially the pastoral:

> A country cottage near a crystal flood
> A winding valley, and a lofty wood.
> Some god conducts me to the sacred shades,
> Where Bacchanals are sung by Spartan maids. . . .
> —Trans. John Dryden

In the Middle Ages people withdrew from the countryside into tiny gardens much as they retreated into walled towns; one such garden with its mixture of flowers and herbs can be seen at the Cloisters in Fort Tryon Park. Dante began his passage through Hell by entering a dark forest; as he left Purgatory he came to a garden, which he described briefly. With the Renaissance the Italians enlarged the garden and, inspired by descriptions of ancient Roman estates, set terraces, fountains and statues on hillsides. Still, the garden remained behind a wall. In seventeenth-century France, André Le Nôtre built vast gardens around palace and château. Making use of the *allée*, originally a way crisscrossing royal forests to guide the hunter, he extended the garden into the distant landscape.

Gardens up to this time were formal; symmetry ruled, often to the last detail. It was not until after 1700 that the English considered abandoning formal planting and having the garden include the countryside, with trees, glades, pastures and water set out in a "natural" or informal manner.

"Why may not a whole estate be thrown into a kind of garden by frequent plantations?" Joseph Addison asked in a *Spectator* paper in 1712, and he added, "A man might make a pretty landskip of his own possessions." Then, as Horace Walpole declared, the architect William Kent "first leaped the fence and saw all nature was a garden" when he designed the grounds of Holkham, a large country house in Norfolk on the North Sea. The fashion gained rapidly in England as landlords enclosed common lands and turned them into private deer parks. The formal, classical gardens that once abounded in England disappeared to become part of the "natural" landscape. In the quest for visual unity even the garden wall was taken down and replaced by a "ha-ha," a concealed ditch, to keep cattle from getting too close to the house. The ha-ha was derived from the concealed trench found in French fortifications of the era, but its name reflects the amusement provoked when it served as a pitfall for the unwary.

The Englishman did not see "nature" as something to be left to its own vagaries. Nor in improving the landscape did he follow his imagination—the word did not even find usage until the Romantic era; he turned to the artist as guide. This was hardly the first time that the artist, especially the painter, had shown the way; the Italian painter of the fifteenth century put the classical city of the Renaissance on canvas before it became stone. The answer to Joseph Addison's question was already on canvas in the work of the seventeenth-century artists Nicolas Poussin, Claude Gelée, known as le Lorrain, and Salvator Rosa. The first two men had painted the countryside of Rome, Virgil's landscape flecked with ancient ruins, a pastoral scene; the third invited the beholder, on the other hand, to look at wild nature. All nature became a picture when seen through the painter's eye:

> Whate'er Lorrain light-touched with softening hue
> Or savage Rosa dashed, or learned Poussin drew.

From painting came the name for the new landscape, the picturesque. It is derived from *pittoresco*, the word Italians adopted to describe "after the manner of painters," specifically the landscape portions of Titian's canvases. The French took it over as *pittoresque*, enlarging the meaning to convey a sense of the strange and the wild. Poussin's "Blind Orion Searching for the Rising Sun," and Claude Lorrain's "St. George and the Dragon" show the landscape that captured the fancy of eighteenth-century England.

Where the hero of the classical landscape of the previous century, the "*jardin de plaisir*," had been Le Nôtre, gardener to Louis XIV, the eighteenth century looked to the Englishman Lancelot Brown. His nickname, "Capability" Brown,

"Blind Orion Searching for the Rising Sun" by Nicolas Poussin. The Italian landscape, as seen by the great French artist, served as model to the English landscape architects of the eighteenth century.

Fletcher Fund, 1924, Metropolitan Museum of Art.

"St. George and the Dragon" is the work of Claude Lorrain, a contemporary of Poussin. He opened men's eyes to the beauties of wild nature, or the picturesque. *Wadsworth Atheneum, Hartford.*

stemmed from his habit of always saying to a prospective client, "Well, my lord, I observe that your park has *great capabilities.*" He was so successful that he refused work in Ireland because he "had not yet finished England." Brown rejected the formal garden, with its straight line, formal bedding, clipped hedge; he demanded the "sublimity" of "rotund forms." For him "beautiful ideas" sprang from the soft lines of carefully tended lawn and meadow, sheets of water in varied outline and soft clumps of tree-filled glades.

> Born to grace Nature, and her works complete
> With all that's beautiful, sublime and great!

For him each Muse enwreathes the Laurel Crown,
And consecrates to Fame immortal Brown.

As in all fashions there were extremes. A favorite ornament of the picturesque for decades was the artificial ruin, Gothic, Chinese or classical. Grottoes were popular. People spoke of "sharawadgi" or a "Chinese" taste for irregularity. When the fashion crossed the Channel to become the *jardin à l'anglaise* and the *englische Garten*, Voltaire, spurning the classical *jardin à la française*, hailed the new fashion:

Jardins, il faut que je vous fuie,
Trop d'art me révolte et m'ennuie,
J'aime mieux ces vastes forêts;

La nature libre et hardie,
Irrégulière dans ses traits,
S'accorde avec ma fantaisie.

And that child of nature Jean-Jacques Rousseau, who planted his own picturesque park, declaimed that "the time has come when we shall want nothing in our gardens but what is found in the countryside." The exported mode was frequently exaggerated; Queen Marie Antoinette built herself a rustic hamlet in the gardens of Versailles, complete with a thatched dairy and cottages where she and her ladies played at milkmaid and shepherdess.

The fever for the picturesque did not rage without check; many pleaded to save some of the old classical formality. A French nobleman mocked the fashion when asked how to lay out a "natural" garden: "Get the gardener drunk and follow him." Among those who protested that the Brown landscape when it matured had a bland quality was Sir Uvedale Price in his *Essays on the Picturesque.* He suggested three varieties of natural landscape: the beautiful, meaning smoothness and gentleness; the sublime, or vastness and obscurity; and the picturesque, or "roughness and sudden variation to irregularity." Of these the last was most important and was to be attained by making use of all natural elements, including rock formations, which Brown had eliminated. The picturesque "is applied to every object and every kind of scenery which has been or might be represented, with good effect in painting . . ." wrote Price. He spoke of "tints of stone and of the soil in broken ground" and of the virtue of water, "a mirror which gives a peculiar freshness and tenderness to the colours it reflects."

Another to rebel against Brown and to exert great influence was the Reverend William Gilpin. While Americans were destroying the forest, Gilpin claimed in his book *Forest Scenery* that "it is no exaggerated praise to call a tree the *grandest* and most *beautiful* of all the productions of the earth." He felt that in picturesque beauty nothing equaled "the form and foliage and ramification of the tree."

The landscape man with the largest practice around 1800 was Humphrey Repton who, while accepting a number of the rebels' suggestions, was the successor of "Capability" Brown. He reintroduced the formal, pointing to "the error of excessive lack of formality round the house." In Brown's landscapes the cows could often look in the window. While Price and Gilpin worshiped the picturesque, Repton sought a balance placing the accent on "neat, simple and elegant effects" to be derived from trees, shrubs, water and turf as *ornaments*. He brought back the use of flowers set in symmetrical bedding. The park of Woburn Abbey, which the present Duke of Bedford has made a major tourist attraction, is Repton's best-known work.

Controversy over landscape design was so strong in England that the issue plays a part in the novels of Jane Austen, Thomas Love Peacock and Benjamin Disraeli. Shelley saw the scenic improvers as "ill-trained beagles . . . snarling at each other when they could not catch the hare." The subject was also much argued over on the Continent.

But while discussion of the picturesque reached hysterical proportions in England and Europe, the subject was barely known in America until well after 1800. The colonial garden was classical, as can be seen in the gardens of Williamsburg. George Washington is generally credited with the first, rare serpentine walk at Mount Vernon. Thomas Jefferson, while he admired the new English landscape, gave no definite pattern to the grounds at Monticello, although they might be defined as vaguely formal. Americans had to await the full impact of romanticism and its glorification of nature before they began "improving" the landscape. The poetry of Wordsworth, to become so popular with Americans, carried the Romantic message, which William Cullen Bryant was one of the first to take up.

> Go forth, under the open sky, and list
> To Nature's teachings . . .

he urged in *Thanatopsis*, published in 1817.

The Romantic Movement found its true home in America in the Hudson Valley; the harbor, the river and the city, in their very dimensions, were made to welcome it. The steamboat had transformed the Hudson into "The Rhine of America"–Robert Fulton's *Clermont* made the first Albany run in 1807; in 1825 Thomas Cole took the trip and founded the Hudson River school of painting. "The painter of American scenes has indeed privileges superior to any other . . . all nature is here new to art," he wrote, finding in the Catskill Mountains scenery "never beheld by Claude [Lorrain] and Salvator [Rosa]. . . ." The New York Public Library still owns Asher B. Durand's "Kindred Spirits," where Cole is seen showing Bryant the beauties of a Catskill ravine. Other painters joined Cole and Durand in depicting the landscape–Thomas Kensett, J. F. Cropsey, Thomas Moran and Frederick E. Church. (The last named became a member of the Park Board in 1871. Church's "Villa Olana," a fine example of the picturesque in architecture, which looks out over the Hudson and the Catskills, has recently been saved from the bulldozer.) John James Audubon, too, should

Thomas Cole showing William Cullen Bryant the wonders of the Catskills in a picture by Asher B. Durand. *New York Public Library.*

be mentioned as helping to excite awareness of a "landscape wholly American; quickened with a life that is real, peculiar to America." He lived in New York from 1839 until his death in 1851.

Playing a humbler role, and one largely forgotten today, was the nurseryman. For years the city had its nurseries, concentrated, for the most part, in what is now the Borough of Queens. The Prince and Parsons nurseries, among the better known, lasted until this century. In the early 1800's Dr. David Hosack's Elgin Botanic Garden was located within the city, occupying the site of Rockefeller Plaza. One nurseryman, Andrew Parmentier of Brooklyn, cousin to the Parmentier who introduced the potato to France, actually prescribed the picturesque in gardening. "Our ancestors," he wrote in 1828, "gave every part of a garden all the exactness of *geometric* forms; they seem to have known no other way to plant trees, except in straight lines, a system totally ruinous to the prospect. Gardens are now treated like landscapes, the charms of which are not to be improved by any rules of art."

The first permanent example of the picturesque in New York is Brooklyn's Green-Wood Cemetery, laid out on the Gowanus Hills in 1839 by Major David B. Douglass. The model was Mount Auburn Cemetery in Cambridge, Massachusetts, dating from 1831, and first of the "garden of graves" indigenous to America. The cemetery was looked on as a pleasure-ground; paying a visit to it on Sunday afternoon became part of the city's ritual.

It was only with Andrew Jackson Downing, already mentioned as one of the chief proponents of a large park for the city, that the science and art of gardening were joined in one person. A citizen of Newburgh, he had begun to landscape estates along the Hudson when, in 1841, he wrote *A Treatise on the Theory and Practice of Landscape Gardening, Adapted to North America: With a View to the Improvement of Country Residences.* The book achieved tremendous popularity. "The *beau ideal*," he wrote, "in Landscape Gardening as a fine art appears to us to be embraced in the creation of scenery expressive of a peculiar kind of beauty, as the elegant or picturesque. . . ." His favorite object was an ornamental tree which, free-standing, he compared to "the Grecian Apollo itself." The banks of the Hudson were especially suited to his end. Here he scattered hemlock, locust, beech and pine, singly and in clumps, on great stretches of turf with invariably a serpentine drive leading to a *cottage orné*, often in Hudson River Gothic or the "bracketed" manner. Little is left of his work save possibly a portion of the Matthew Vassar estate at Poughkeepsie, now part of the women's college. (A one-time associate of Downing, Alexander Jackson Davis, laid out an early Romantic suburban park of 1,400 acres in West Orange, New Jersey, in 1853. Llewellyn Park still exists and, interestingly, a jointly owned strip of park land has the name "Ramble," through which flows a waterway similar to the one found in the northern end of Central Park.)

Mostly due to the agitation of Downing and Bryant, creation of a large park became a political issue in New York by 1850. During the mayoralty campaign of that year both candidates came out for one, and in 1851, the winner, Mayor Ambrose C. Kingsland, asked the Common Council to take action. That worthy body recommended Jones Wood, 153½ acres bounded by Third Avenue and the East River from 66th to 75th streets. The State Legislature, where real power still resides in such matters, confirmed the choice. Downing, who had very definite ideas on what a park should be, at once protested the size and site in *The Horticulturist* of August, 1851:

> Five hundred acres *is the smallest area that should be reserved for the future wants of such a city*, now, *while it may be obtained. Five hundred acres may be selected between 39th Street and the Harlem River, including a varied*

> *surface of land, a good deal of which is yet waste area, so that the whole may be purchased at something like a million of dollars. In that area there would be space enough to have broad reaches of park and pleasure-grounds, with a real feeling of the breadth and beauty of green fields, the perfume and freshness of nature. In its midst would be located the great distributing reservoirs of the Croton aqueduct, formed into lovely lakes of limpid water, covering many acres, and heightening the charm of the sylvan accessories by the finest natural contrast. In such a park, the citizens who would take excursions in carriages, or on horseback, could have the substantial delights of country roads and country scenery, and forget for a time the rattle of the pavements and the glare of brick walls. Pedestrians would find quiet and secluded walks when they wished to be solitary, and broad alleys filled with thousands of happy faces, when they would be gay. The thoughtful denizen of the town would go out there in the morning to hold converse with the whispering trees, and the wearied tradesmen in the evening, to enjoy an hour of happiness by mingling in the open spaces with "all the world."*

In other words, Central Park. A year after he wrote this, Downing, only thirty-seven, drowned in the Hudson, rescuing his mother-in-law in a gruesome steamboat disaster off Riverdale. Had he lived he would have designed the new park.

In 1853 the State Legislature authorized the city to buy the site from 59th to 106th streets between Fifth and Eighth avenues, some 624 acres. A Commission of Estimate and Assessment was appointed to acquire the land. For a brief moment there seemed a chance that the city would also buy Jones Wood. But besides the objections to its limited extent there was the opposition of businessmen, among them those who felt that none of the riverbank "ought ever to be taken from the purposes of commerce, as the whole will eventually be acquired, including the ground now known as the Battery." This opposition reflected the businessman's curious fear of surrendering river and harbor banks to public pleasure, a fear common to all American cities and towns in the last century. The four sides of good taxable property that Central Park would provide appealed to business, and besides, some of the land was already public property. There were in addition the 10 acres of state-owned land around the Arsenal (built in 1848), 37 1/2 acres occupied by the old Croton Reservoir (site of the Great Lawn) completed in 1842, and 106 acres purchased in 1852 as site for the New or present Reservoir, also known when first built as Lake Manhattan. In selecting park land around its water system the city was following a general pattern; Fairmount Park in Philadelphia, the largest public park within an American city, had its start in 1855 at the Fairmount Water Works on the banks of the Schuylkill. In all probability the Hudson River Valley will be conserved because New York and other cities are dependent on the river water.

One last important element in the present site's favor was that its size made possible lengthy carriage drives. The amateurs of driving had been among those demanding a large public park. "As a metropolis of wealth and fashion, New York has one great deficiency—that of a *driving park*," wrote Nathaniel P. Willis as early as 1844. "Rome has its Pincian Hill, Florence its Cascine, Paris its Bois de Boulogne, and London its Hyde Park. . . . Such a place is only *not* considered indispensable in New York because it has never been enjoyed." Unquestionably, Central Park did make driving fashionable. Anticipating the trend, Brewster and Company opened a factory in 1856 in a building still standing on the northwest corner of Broome and Mott streets and became the city's greatest carriage maker.

Despite the legislation passed in 1853, the project faced obstacles. The Common Council voted in 1855 to reduce the size of the park, lopping off the section from 59th to 72nd streets. Acting for once in the public interest, Mayor Fernando Wood vetoed the resolution. The next year, after the report of the Commission of Estimate and Assessment had been confirmed, the city took title to the land. By 1859 it was decided that the park should be enlarged to include the land from 106th to 110th streets. With its acquisition total acreage came to 843 acres, the cost of the land coming to about five million dollars, a million and a half of which was assessed on owners of property adjacent to the park.

A commission for the management of Central Park was appointed in 1856, and a Board of Commissioners of the Park was established by an act of the legislature in 1857. Assisting the commissioners was an Advisory Committee, which included the historian George Bancroft, the newspaperman Charles A. Dana and the writer Washington Irving as president. Egbert L. Vielé was named Chief Engineer of the new park. Later a brigadier general in the Union Army, Vielé today is best known as the author of the *Topographical Atlas of the City of New York*, which for years has been used by construction men to locate forgotten springs, streams and swamps. (His youngest son, Francis Vielé-Griffin, 1863–1937, became a French symbolist poet and would have been appointed to the French Academy had he not insisted on retaining his American citizenship.)

The park gained its strongest administrative defender in 1857 when Andrew Haswell Green was elected Treasurer of the Park Board. A lawyer by profession, closely associated with the Democratic leader Samuel J. Tilden, Green was one of the outstanding New Yorkers of the last century. Endowed with unusual energy and a Roman sense of civic responsibility, he let little escape his attention in matters beneficial to the city. The designers of Central Park were to have many differences with Green, but it was he who fought the battles in the noisy political arena. (For more on Green, see the Northern Tour.)

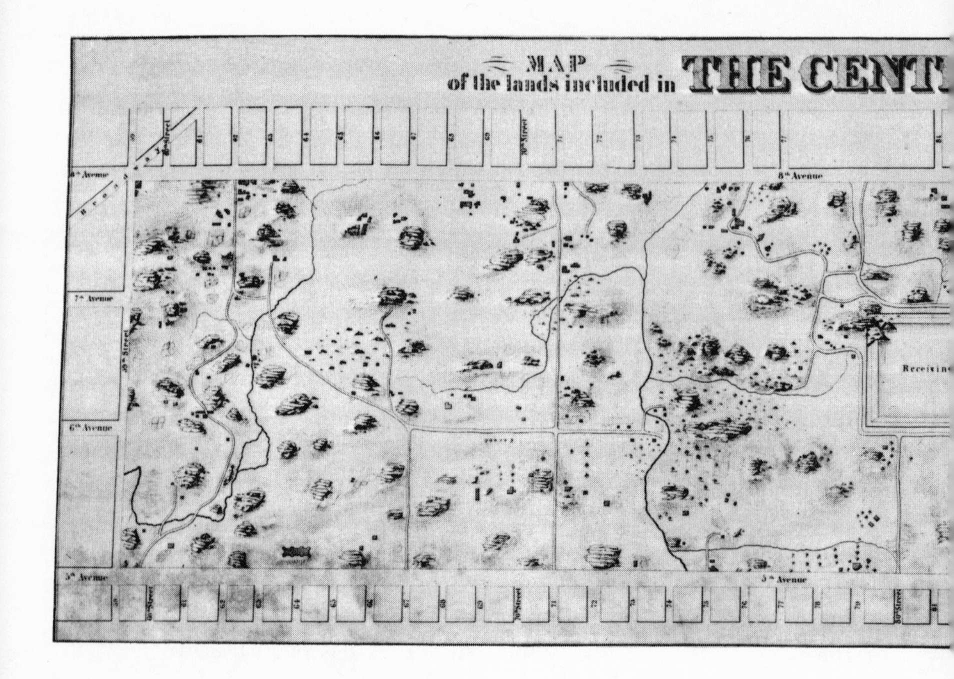

The topographical survey of the Central Park lands made by the engineer, Egbert L. Viele in 1856. It shows the desolation of the site. "Seneca Village," a squatters' hamlet, is just west of the Old Receiving Reservoir. *New York Public Library.*

One of the early acts of the Park Commissioners was to persuade the Croton Aqueduct Board to change its rectangular plan for the New Reservoir to one following the natural contours it still has. The work of clearing the park site began on August 12, 1857.

The stage was now set for the two principals. The first to appear was Frederick Law Olmsted who, it might be said, sidled crabwise onto the scene. Finishing a book at a seaside resort, he ran into a Park Commissioner who suggested he apply for the job of Park Superintendent, the man in charge of clearing and construction. Olmsted agreed to apply and returned to the city that night to find backers. Those who

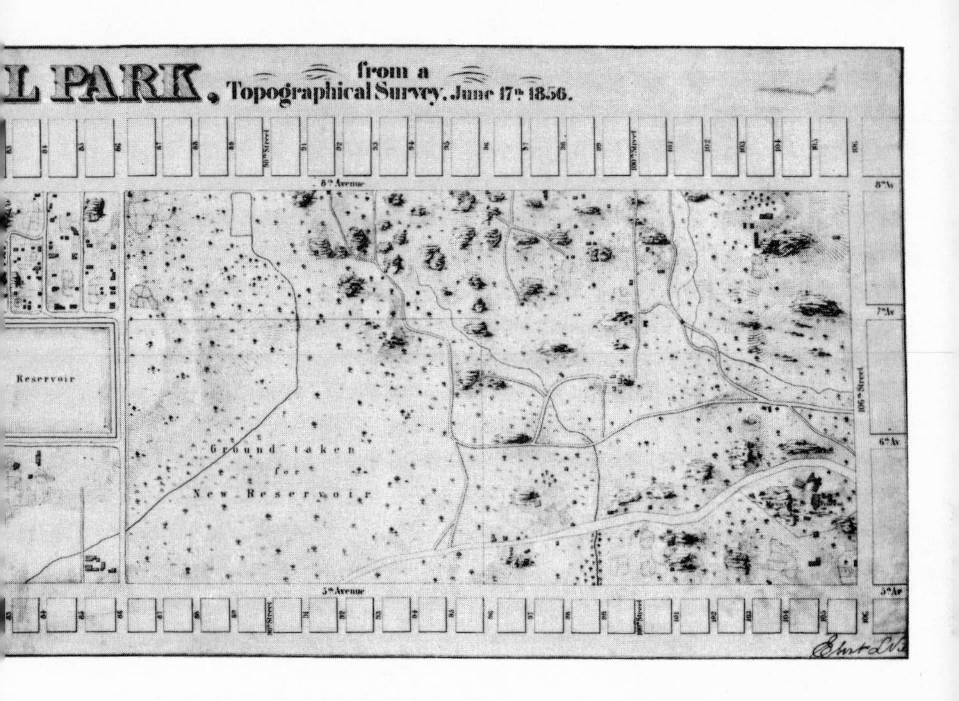

signed his petition included Horace Greeley, William Cullen Bryant, August Belmont, Asa Gray, the famous botanist, and Washington Irving. Olmsted's background was that of the passionate amateur, a point that put off the commissioners looking for a "practical man." However, Irving's signature won him the job.

The land that became Olmsted's province must have been a discouraging sight, filled as it was with squatters' shacks, bone-boiling works, "swill-mills" and hog farms, offering a spectacle not too different from the one still to be seen in the Jersey meadows from turnpike and railroad. Interspersed among the swamps, creeks which were open sewers, and bramble-covered grounds were no less than three hundred hovels. Olmsted summed up the site as "a pestilential spot, where rank vegetation and miasmatic odors taint every breath of air." The squatters fought back against the park workers trying to eject them, and the police had to be called in to do the job. To complicate matters a panic descended on the nation in 1857, and work on the site was looked on by the political chieftains as a relief program for deserving ward heelers. Olmsted's job was made doubly difficult by the fact that his reputation as an amateur had preceded him. In spite of this personal nuisance and the constant interference of city and state officials demanding favors, he was able to tell his father in the early part of 1858: "I have got the park into a capital discipline, a perfect system, working like a machine —1,000 men now at work." That the men came to have pride in the project is evidenced by their participation in the parade celebrating the laying of the transatlantic cable in August, 1858. "The workmen, attired in their everyday clothes, with evergreens in their hats, next marched in squads of four, each gang carrying a banner with the name of their boss-workmen inscribed thereon," reported *The Tribune*.

> *In the line of the procession were several four-horse teams drawing wagons in which were the workmen in the engineer's department. On the sides of the vehicles were muslin banners with the words: ENGINEER CORPS. . . . The procession filled Broadway from Union Square to the Park [City Hall Park], and, as it was altogether unexpected, it created no little excitement and inquiry. If all the men and teams in this turnout are kept at the city's work, we shall soon see great improvement in the new park. . . .*

Although he was superintendent, Olmsted had no idea of extending the power of his office to designing a plan for the park; his job was to clear the ground. Even when the commission announced a competition for a park design in October, 1857, he gave no thought to competing until Calvert Vaux, an architect, suggested that they collaborate. Still Olmsted hesitated, thinking that Vielé, his superior, who had already prepared a plan for the park, might frown on the effort; only after Vielé offered no objection did Olmsted accept Vaux's invitation. The two men submitted their plan on April 1, 1858, under the signature "Greensward"; on April 28, Greensward was declared the best of the thirty-three competing plans.

If one were to treat Olmsted's life cavalierly, there would be little to indicate, at least in the first years, that he would become America's greatest landscape architect. Born in 1822, the son of a Hartford, Connecticut, merchant, he was forced to interrupt his studies at Yale because of eye trouble. Outdoor life seemed the best corrective, and his father bought him a farm outside of New Haven and then, in 1848, another on Staten Island where the young man also had a nursery. He went to England in 1850 to observe farming methods and while there made a special effort to see public parks. On his return he wrote of his experiences in *Walks and Talks of an American Farmer in England.* Next he made several trips through the South, sending back descriptions to *The New York Times*, subsequently published in *A Journey in the Slave States*, *A Journey in Texas* and *A Journey in the Back Country*, which, together, form a prime historical source of conditions in the pre-Civil War South. He even tried his hand at publishing and editing, a venture that left him with the debts that influenced his decision to accept Vaux's suggestion to enter the park competition with its $2,000 prize.

But Olmsted was not satisfied with being a moderately successful journalist; from boyhood his interest in the landscape had amounted to a passion. "I can see that my pleasure began to be affected by conditions of scenery at an early age," he recalled, "–long before it could have been suspected by others from anything that I said and before I began to mentally connect the cause and effect of enjoyment in it." Reading Virgil he was first introduced to the pastoral, a concept he was to adopt for America's great urban parks. He remembered discovering in the Hartford Public Library "Price on the *Pictur-*

esque and Gilpin on *Forest Scenery*—books of the last century, but which I esteem so much more than any published since, as stimulating the exercise of judgement in matters of my art." When he settled on Staten Island in 1848 he contributed to Downing's magazine, *The Horticulturist.* When he went abroad, Downing gave him letters to English colleagues, and he dedicated *Walks and Talks* to Downing's memory. On his own and his neighbors' farms on Staten Island. Olmsted had undertaken some landscaping, "as any fairly well-to-do, working farmer may. . . ." As to a specific interest in public parks, he was to write to Vaux with that serious and, perhaps, humorless tone that was so characteristic of the man:

> *that this was something deeper than a whim you know, for you know that it existed essentially years before it attached itself to the Central Park as was shown by the fact that while others gravitated to pictures, architecture, Alps, libraries, high life and low life when travelling, I had gravitated to parks,—spent all my spare time in them, when living in London for instance, and this with no purpose whatever except a gratification which came from sources which the Superintendence of the Park would have made easy and cheap to me to say the least, every day of my life. What I wanted in London and in Paris and in Brussels and everywhere I went in Europe—what I wanted in New York in 1857, I want now and this from no regard for Art or fame or money.*

Unlike his collaborator, Calvert Vaux was a professional. Born in London in 1824, he was apprenticed while quite young to a leading architectural firm. In the summer of 1850 he met Downing, who had gone abroad to study parks and to seek an architectural partner. He was hired, came to America the same year with the landscape man and went to work in Downing's Newburgh office. The commissions he worked on included the landscaping for the National Capitol and for the Smithsonian Institution. He stayed on in Newburgh after Downing's death in 1852, practicing his profession, and married a local girl. In 1857, the year his book *Villas and Cottages: A Series of Designs Prepared for Execution in the United States* was published, Vaux moved to New York. Then came the work on the Greensward plan, done mostly at his house at 136 East 18th Street.

> *When the drawing of the plan of Central Park to go into the competition was being made at my father's house in 18th Street, in conjunction with Mr. Frederick Law Olmsted* [his son recalled], *there was a great deal of grass to be put in by the usual small dots and dashes, and it became the friendly thing for callers to help on the work by joining in and adding some grass to Central Park.*

The two men worked together, usually on Sundays and at night, as Olmsted was occupied with his superintendency during the day. They explored the ground that Olmsted knew so well, talking over every part of it to the last detail before coming to any decision. Nothing is known of the actual manner of collaboration, nor of what each brought to the design, but judging from the documents that survive on Brooklyn's Prospect Park, designed by the two men in 1866, Vaux's role was as decisive as Olmsted's. In fact, the former seems often to have been the moving force, for in 1865, when Olmsted had temporarily abandoned the profession, Vaux wrote to him arguing that he return: "You do not quite see that now your artistic capacities are the most needed. The country wants artists. . . . I have upheld your art position [vis-à-vis the Commissioners] as well as I knew how and have done enough to show you that success is possible. In the next twenty years Landscape Architecture is the thing needed as much as anything." And it was Vaux who drew the first plans for Prospect Park and persuaded Olmsted to join in the work.

A great city park was called for, the stage was set and the right men came forward. Olmsted and Vaux were moved by a rare mixture of idealism, passion, and maturity of vision.

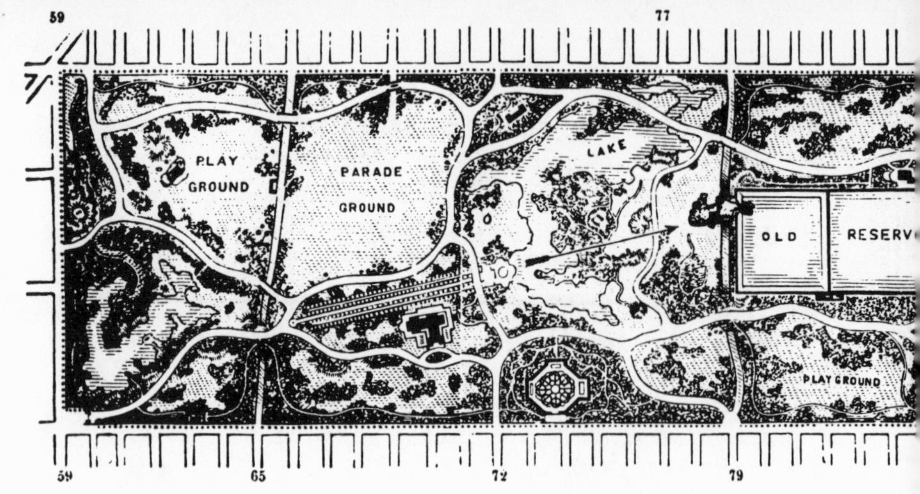

FIRST STUDY OF DESIG

The top map is the Greensward plan that won the competition in 1858. It stopped at 106th Street. The lower map, dating from 1868, shows the extension north to 110th Street. Among the changes that Frederick Law Olmsted and Calvert Vaux made in carrying out the work was the substitution of Conservatory Water for a formal garden.

New-York Historical Society.

Their design for Central Park gave the picturesque a new dimension, placing it in the public domain. A landscape style, initiated in eighteenth-century England, which had spread throughout Europe settled in mid-nineteenth-century Amer-

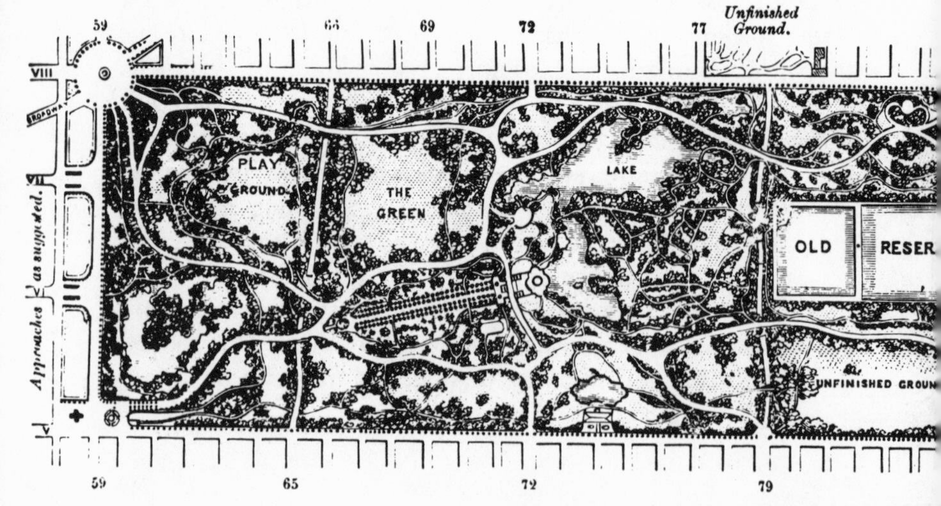

MAP OF TH

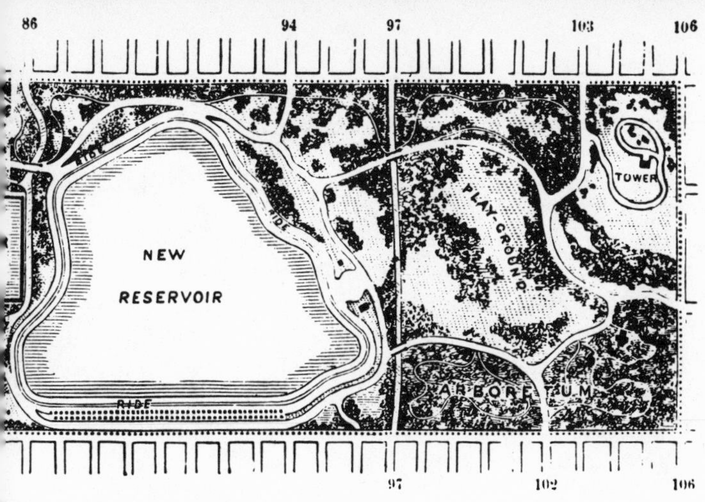

'OR THE CENTRAL PARK.

ica. It was here that the picturesque landscape was to know its last great stage, shaping city park and suburb. By the 1900's the style had gone out of fashion and today survives only in an emasculated form.

The key to the Greensward plan lay "in adopting the actual situation to its purpose. . . ." The designers considered the park to fall naturally into two sections, upper and lower, with

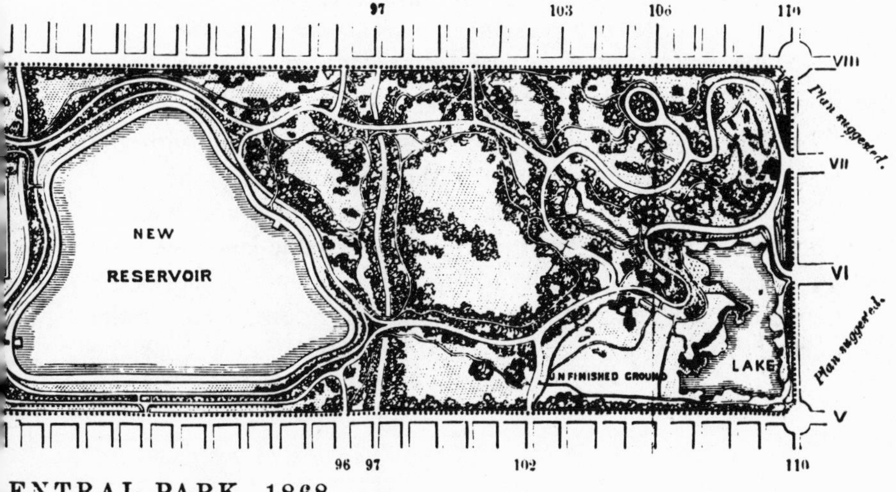

ENTRAL PARK, 1868.

the dividing line at what is now the 85th Street Transverse Road.

The horizon lines of the upper park [*they wrote*], *are bold and sweeping and the slopes have great breadth in almost every aspect in which they may be contemplated. As this character is the highest ideal that can be aimed at for a park under any circumstances, and as it is in most decided contrast to the confined and formal lines of the city it is desirable to interfere with it, by crossroads and other constructions, as little as possible. Formal planting and architectual effects, unless on a very grand scale, must be avoided. . . .*

They saw the lower park—and it is interesting to follow them across the then unsightly desert—as "far more heterogeneous in its character" requiring "much more varied treatment."

The most important feature in its landscape, [*they continued*], *is the long rocky and wooded hill-side lying immediately south of the Reservoir.* [*The hillside is the one now crowned by the towered Belvedere, and the reservoir referred to the old one, which occupied the site of the Great Lawn until 1929.*] *Inasmuch as beyond this point there do not appear to be any leading natural characteristics of similar consequence in the scenery, it will be important to draw as much attention as possible to this hill-side, to afford facilities for rest and leisurely contemplation upon the rising ground opposite and to render the lateral boundaries of the park in its vicinity as inconspicuous as possible.*

This they did by placing the Lake to the south with the Terrace facing the hillside to the north and by siting the Mall on the Terrace-hillside axis. "The central and western portion of the lower park is an irregular table-land; the eastern is composed of a series of graceful undulations, suggesting lawn or gardenesque treatment." And they concluded, "in the extreme south we find some flat alluvial meadow; but the general character of the ground is rugged and there are several bold, rocky bluffs, that help to give individuality to this part of the composition." This is the essence of the *picturesque*, as defined by the English landscape men, Repton and Price, achieved by taking full advantage of natural features of the site—hillocks, rock formations, flat ground and hollows.

The long, narrow shape of the park presented problems to the designers, and so did the two adjacent reservoirs in the central portion. Occupying one-sixth of the park's area, or 143 acres, the reservoirs restricted landscaping to narrow borders running south-north from 79th Street almost to 96th.

The drives were to run north-south, dictated by the rectangular shape of the park as well as by the two reservoirs. The walks and drives, and later the bridle path, were placed in such a way that, by means of bridges and tunnels, pedestrian crossings were kept to a minimum. Olmsted and Vaux were the first to introduce the contemporary notion of traffic separation on a large scale, an invention that "Capability" Brown had devised a century before for a private English park. As for east-west traffic, a serious problem, they provided four sunken transverse roads that in no way interfered with the over-all design. An amusing coda to the Greensward text was the designers' explanation for the twisting drives, the bane of car drivers:

> *It will be perceived that no long straight drive has been provided on the plan; this feature has been studiously avoided, because it would offer opportunities for trotting matches. The popular idea of the park is a beautiful open space, in which quiet drives, rides, and strolls may be had. This cannot be preserved if a race-course, or a road that can readily be used as a race-course, is made one of its leading attractions.*

The hot-rodders of the day were the fast trotters who, in the late 1850's, clustered daily on what is now Broadway in the neighborhood of 90th Street; they were a nuisance that had to be barred from the park.

Other than the plan itself, permanently exhibited on the third floor of the Arsenal, and the explanatory text, the presentation of Greensward was accompanied by before-and-after views, a device that Humphrey Repton made popular. In contrast, the other competitors came forward with earnest and unimaginative efforts. Most of their plans were fussy versions of suburban gardens, filled with squiggly paths and raised flower beds in the shape of the city's coat of arms or similar patterns. The most patriotic of them featured a series of fountains. In one there was to be a statue of the Goddess of Liberty, an emblematic eagle on her left shoulder and thirteen currents of water gushing forth from under her feet, "denoting the thirteen old states, whose independence sprang up under the footsteps of the goddess." Another, celebrating the then existing States of the Union, had thirty-two waterspouts falling into a basin from the center of which was to rise a statue of George Washington pouring water from a cup in his right hand, a crown lying at his feet. "The illustrious hero," the plan's designer explained, "magnanimously rejected a crown which was within his grasp, and preferred to pour out, like a living stream of water, the rich blessing of liberty over the land he had redeemed from bondage by his indomitable energy, and preserved from anarchy by his profound wisdom."

The commissioners approved Olmsted and Vaux's plan, but several of them asked for the elimination of the sunken transverse roads! Today this practical device is the one that receives the most praise, although its example is seldom followed, at least in city planning—but ours is a "practical age." They also suggested a straight promenade avenue running south-north in the middle of the park from 59th to 79th streets. This included a towered suspension bridge at one point. Fortunately neither proposal won acceptance. One important suggestion of the commissioners was adopted: the bridle path, originally confined to a circuit of the New Reservoir, was expanded south and north.

It must not be assumed that Olmsted and Vaux, once having made the changes in Greensward called for by the commissioners, then followed their plan to the letter.

> *In view of the great beauty of this park* [*was one summation of their work*], *it is instructive to know that none was ever created in a less theoretical, in a more practical way—less in the office, more in the open air. The design of Messrs. Olmsted and Vaux, as first drawn and accepted, was very different from their design as we see it realized today. The former was, of course, adapted after careful study to the very peculiar and difficult site in view. But during the long years while the actual work progressed, it was perpetually modified in deference to the minuter knowledge gained by its creators. They lived on the borders of the park and studied its face as a portrait painter studies the face of his sitter. Day by day they reviewed and revised their proposed emendations on the site itself. Thus a great work of art was achieved, and thus only can a great work of landscape art ever be achieved—"through patiently extended experiments upon the spot itself."*

They were but following the dictum of Alexander Pope in his *Moral Essay* dedicated to the great Lord Burlington:

> In all, let Nature never be forgot.
> But treat the Goddess like a modest fair,
> Nor over-dress, nor leave her wholly bare;
> Let not each beauty ev'ry where be spy'd,
> Where half the skill is decently to hide.
> He gains all points, who pleasingly confounds,
> Surprizes, varies, and conceals the Bounds.
> Consult the Genius of the Place in all;
> That tells the Waters or to rise, or fall;
> Or helps th' ambitious Hill the heav'ns to scale,
> Or scoops in circling theatres the Vale;
> Calls in the Country, catches op'ning glades,

Joins willing woods, and varies shades from shades;
Now breaks, or now directs, th' intending Lines;
Paints as you plant, and, as you work, designs.

Nature in Manhattan in 1858 was hardly the Goddess fair; she was a grubby, unkempt urchin in need of far more than a bath. After Greensward took the prize, Olmsted, continuing as Superintendent, became Architect-in-Chief and Vaux, Assistant to the Architect-in-Chief. Work on the park, begun in 1857, went on at a faster pace. Loads of loose rock continued to be removed and used to fashion a temporary park wall; the drained swamps were cleared and several basins made ready for water. To carry out the Greensward design tremendous jobs of blasting and filling had to be done. Up to the end of 1873, 4,825,000 cubic yards of stone, earth and topsoil (amounting to 10,000,000 one-horse cartloads) were moved out of or into the park. The original soil, a glacial outwash with little organic matter, was treated with fertilizer and top soil, 500,039 cubic yards of the latter being spread in the park from 1858 to 1865.

Paths, drives, bridges and transverse roads were built, and drainage, a key part of any park, seldom considered because invisible, took the form of sixty-two miles of earthenware drainage pipe. Irrigation was provided by hydrants placed along the drives and on the lawns. Twelve and one-half miles of water pipe were laid by 1861. The first tree was planted in the park on October 17, 1858. For reasons of economy, two nurseries with 25,000 trees were established on park land. Most of the seedlings came from nurseries then on the city's periphery, although some were imported from Scotland; 17,300 trees and shrubs were set out in 1859, 16,200 in 1860, 52,700 in 1861, 74,730 in 1862—figures that indicate the extent of the operation. By 1873 it was estimated that, all told, four to five million trees, shrubs and vines had been planted. Only 42 species of trees were found growing on the park site prior to the clearing; by 1873 there were 402 species of deciduous

A view of the Arsenal from the south in 1862. Fifth Avenue is to the right. The Zoo now fills the left portion of the picture. The Denesmouth Bridge, in the background, stands just south of the present Children's Zoo. *Photo Victor Prevost. Stuart Collection, New York Public Library.*

trees and shrubs, 149 nonconiferous evergreens and "American" plants in open ground, 81 conifers, and 815 hardy perennials and alpines.

Sharing responsibility for the park's planting was Ignaz Anton Pilat, 1820–1870, an Austrian who had studied at the Imperial Botanical Gardens at Schönbrunn in Vienna. One of the many political refugees of 1848, he worked first in the South, later moving to New York. Like Olmsted and Vaux he dedicated himself to Central Park. While the designers no doubt laid down the main lines of planting, the choice and siting of the varieties devolved on Pilat. Judging from the 1873 plant list, he favored use of quite a few subtropical broad-leafed plants so popular in the last century. Other than the attempt to emphasize native trees and shrubs, the most interesting aspect of the planting was the extensive use of evergreens, essential to give color to the park in winter. They included a large number of conifers, not only a wide variety of pine but also fir, spruce, cedar (including the cedar of Lebanon), hemlock, and juniper. Evergreens were planted throughout the park, but were found in greatest number along the West Drive from 77th Street north to 100th Street, the stretch referred to as the "Winter Drive."

The park was immediately popular from the moment a portion of it was opened in the fall of 1858. As the landscaping spread north from 59th Street, visitors came in growing numbers. George Templeton Strong, the diarist who saw and recorded everything going on in the city, was among the early explorers.

> *Improved the day by leaving Wall Street early [he wrote on June 11, 1859], and set off with George Anthon and Johnny to explore the Central Park, which will be a feature of the city within five years and a lovely place in* A.D. *1900, when its trees will have acquired dignity and appreciable diameters. Perhaps the city itself will perish before then, by growing too big to live under faulty institutions corruptly administered. Reached the park a little before four, just as the red flag was hoisted—the signal for the blasts of the day. They were all around us for some twenty minutes, now booming far off to the north, now quite near, now distant again, like a desultory "affair" between advanced posts of two great armies. We entered the park at Seventy-first Street, on its east side, and made for "The Ramble,"*

a patch just below the upper reservoir [the Old Reservoir]. Its footpaths and plantations are finished, more or less, and it is the first section of the ground that has been polished off and made presentable. It promises very well. So does all the lower park, though now in most ragged condition: long lines of incomplete macadamization, "lakes" without water, mounds of compost, piles of blasted stone, acres of what may be greensward hereafter but is now mere brown earth; groves of slender young transplanted maples and locusts, undecided between life and death, with here and there an arboricultural experiment that has failed utterly and is a mere broomstick with ramifications. Celts, caravans of dirt carts, derricks, steam engines, these are the elements out of which our future Pleasaunce is rapidly developing. The work seems pushed with vigor and system, and as far as it has gone, looks thorough and substantial. . . . Narrowness is its chief drawback. One sees quite across this Rus in Urbe *at many points. This will be less felt as the trees grow. The tract seems to have been judiciously laid out. Roads and paths twist about in curves of artistic tortuosity. A broad avenue, exceptionally straight . . . [the Mall] with a quadruple row of elms, will look Versailles-y by* A.D. *1950. . . .*

Oliver Wendell Holmes was another early visitor. "The Autocrat of the Breakfast Table" stopped off in the city while taking home his son, Captain Oliver Wendell Holmes, Jr., of the 20th Massachusetts, wounded a second time at Antietam.

The Central Park is an expanse of wild country [observed the elder Holmes in 1862], well crumpled so as to form ridges which will give views and hollows that will hold water. The hips and elbows and other bones of Nature stick out here and there in the shape of rocks which give character to the scenery, and an unchangeable, unpurchasable look to a landscape that without them would have been in danger of being fattened by art and money out of all its native features. The roads were fine, the sheets of water beautiful, the bridges handsome, the swans elegant in their deportment, the grass green and as short as a fast horse's winter coat. I could not learn whether it was kept so by clipping or singeing. I was delighted with my new property,—but it cost me four dollars to get there [from 23rd Street and Fifth Avenue], so far was it beyond the Pillars of Hercules of the fashionable quarter.

In the 1860's there were many vacant lots south of 59th Street, and the land adjacent to the park was almost completely unimproved. Had Holmes returned in 1876, when the park was considered completed, he would no doubt have been astonished to see how far north the city had advanced.

Holmes's delight in Central Park reflected the delight of all, and in the last year of the Civil War visitors numbered over seven million. The charm and novelty of the setting that by then was the city's chief attraction was accented by the presence of deer and sheep. The herd of deer soon disappeared but, for years, the presence of sheep made the park seem almost exotic in contrast to the commercial and industrial city.

Before the park opened some people and notably the press had worried about who would use the park and how they would behave. The *Herald* had declared in 1858 that it would be nothing but "a great bear-garden for the lowest denizens of the city." A few years later, however, in a drastic change of opinion, the newspaper crowed:

When one is inclined to despair of the country, let him go to the Central Park on a Saturday, and spend a few hours there in looking at the people—not at those who come in gorgeous carriages, but at those who arrive on foot, or in those exceedingly democratic conveyances, the street-cars. . . . We regret to say that the more brilliant becomes the display of vehicles and toilettes, the more shameful is the display of bad manners on the part of the extremely fine-looking people who ride in carriages and wear fine dresses. We must add that the pedestrians always behave well.

The pedestrians' good behavior and the respectful attitude the public at large showed for the park did not evolve of themselves but were responses conditioned largely by the efforts of Olmsted. "A large part of the people of New York," he wrote in 1857, "are ignorant of a park. . . . They will need to be trained to the proper use of it, to be restrained in the abuse of it." One of his duties as superintendent was the organization of a special police force, called "Park-Keepers," in 1858. He also drew up a list of regulations, which were posted around the park and enforced by the Park-Keepers. They included restrictions against walking on the grass, except lawns bearing the sign "Common," damaging the landscape in any way, molesting birds, or turning loose in the park domestic animals, any animals, for that matter. Dogs were required to be kept on a leash no longer than five feet in length.

Olmsted's concern for the park went far beyond concern with Park-Keepers; he wanted control over every detail of management as well as design. The control he demanded led, of course, to conflict with the Park Commissioners, especially with the park's financial watchdog, Andrew Haswell Green. With the outbreak of the Civil War, Olmsted obtained a leave of absence to accept an appointment as secretary to what became the United States Sanitary Commission, the predecessor of the American Red Cross. In 1863 both he and Vaux handed in the first of several resignations, so strong were their differences with the Park Commissioners. A year later Olmsted still chafed at the memory of what he called Green's "systematic small tyranny . . . he was slow murder." Yet in 1865 Green was largely responsible for the designers' being rehired as landscape architects. Olmsted was reluctant to return to the park, partly because he had been asked to join the staff of the newly launched *Nation* but, as mentioned before, Vaux convinced his partner not to give up landscape architecture.

Even the Civil War did not stop work on the park. In 1863 title was taken to the northern addition, and the Loch was completed in 1865, Harlem Meer a year later. The few buildings placed in the park under the supervision of the designers, all designed by Vaux, were constructed in this period; the only ones left are Belvedere Castle (1871), the Dairy (1870), which lost its porch in the 1950's, the Central Park Precinct Station (1871), and the Workshops (1871). The oldest buildings in the park are the 1814 Blockhouse, the Arsenal, dating from 1848, and the two gate houses of the Reservoir, built in 1863.

Olmsted and Vaux were slow to recognize the dangers structures represented, for they were initially eager to foster educational enterprises in the park. They had reserved the Arsenal in the Greensward Plan for museum use, and the upper floor provided cramped quarters for the American Museum of Natural History from 1869 to 1877. Fortunately a place for that wonderful institution was found in Manhattan Square on the western edge of the park. The Menagerie, or Zoo, the designers felt, had no place within the park, but the Park Commissioners decided differently. As for the Metropolitan Museum of Art, its site had been set aside for institutional use by the State Legislature in 1868. Olmsted and Vaux did not at first object to this siting, but as the years went by and the museum expanded in all directions they realized their error. (The addition of an acre parking lot in 1957 brought the museum's total acreage to about 12.5.) The Prospect Park commissioners, managing things better, set aside land outside their park for institutional use; consequently, the Brooklyn park is not covered by buildings continually threatening to expand. "Building can be brought within the business of the Park proper only as it will aid escape from building," Olmsted stated clearly in 1882. "Where building for other purpose begins, there the park ends. The reservoirs and the museum are not a part of the Park proper: They are deductions from it."

Another threat to the park took the form of statuary. As a dumping-ground the park exerted great attraction. The first statue, a female figure representing Commerce, came in 1865; it has disappeared, but many of the others are all too present.

The daily struggle of Olmsted and Vaux to stand off encroachments upon the greensward was not made any easier by shifts in politics. Boss Tweed succeeded in driving Andrew Haswell Green out of office in the spring of 1870, and the two landscape men were forced to resign that fall. Under the so-called Tweed Charter, which was the first to give the municipality some real power, the old Board of the Commissioners of Central Park was abolished and a new board of five, appointed by the mayor, came to head a new Department of Public Parks. (The organization remained practically unchanged until the Greater New York Charter of 1897.) With Tweed's downfall in 1871 the two designers were back again, horrified at the destruction done in the name of correcting "neglect."

> *In parts of the Park in which intricacy and low growth and picturesque obscurity had been required by the design* [*ran their report*], *the natural underwood has been grubbed up, the original admirably rugged surface made as smooth and meadow-like as ledge-rock would allow, and the trees, to a height of from ten to fifteen feet, trimmed to bare poles.... No shrubbery or low growth seems to have been valued unless it could be seen within a clean-edged dug border.*

In more recent years the same has been done as a "crime-deterrent," plant life being always singled out as inviting the malevolent.

Another legacy of the Tweed regime, and equally serious as it was long-lasting, was the lapse in discipline among the Park-Keepers. In 1876 Green was out of office, this time permanently. Two years later Olmsted was dismissed, and in 1883 Vaux resigned. For Olmsted dismissal brought a break with the city. Although he had been living at 209 West 46th Street, his work was taking him increasingly to Massachusetts, and he abandoned New York in 1883, taking up residence in Brookline, a suburb of Boston. "For ten years past I have been sick of New York," he complained to Vaux in 1887—a familiar cry. "Its infernal politics had wrought the most intense and ruinous disappointment with me. . . . I left New York only because I was sick of it—its Park Commission and its infernal underground politics and after coming here I diligently cut myself away from New York and its associations. . . ."

The two men had had an active partnership after the Civil War. Following their appointment as landscape architects to Prospect Park in 1866, came such commissions as the original campus of the University of California at Berkeley; the development of Riverside, outside Chicago; a park in Buffalo as well as several in Chicago; and Riverside and Morningside parks in New York. The firm broke up in 1872, and Olmsted pursued his triumphant career with Mount Royal Park in Montreal; the National Capitol grounds in Washington; the Boston park system; Belle Isle Park in Detroit; the site plan for the World's Columbian Exposition of 1893; the Kansas City park system; the vast grounds of the George W. Vanderbilt estate, "Biltmore," outside of Asheville, N. C., and many others. His business was inherited by his sons; the firm continued vigorously in Brookline as Olmsted Brothers, until recent years.

Vaux remained in New York, serving as Landscape Architect to the Park Department from 1881 to 1883 and again from 1888 until he drowned in Gravesend Bay in 1895.

Vaux's successor was Samuel B. Parsons, Jr., son and grandson of leading Flushing nurserymen. (His father is still recalled as author of *The Rose: Its History, Poetry, Culture and Classification*, reprinted many times as *Parsons on the Rose.*) A graduate of Yale, young Parsons began his landscaping career working for Vaux and, from 1880 to 1882, the two men were partners. Like his father, he turned author, writing *Landscape Gardening* and *Landscape Gardening Studies*, which contain descriptions of Central Park. For fifteen years he was Superintendent of Parks and, from 1901 to 1911, Landscape Architect to the Department. It was in the course of his tenure that, with the coming of Greater New York on January 1, 1898, the Board of Commissioners was reduced from four to three members, one for Manhattan and Richmond, one for the Bronx and one for Brooklyn and Queens. In 1911 Queens obtained a separate commissioner, and in 1920 Richmond received the same, raising the board to five, one for each borough.

Parsons' departure from the Department of Parks in 1911 signaled the close of the "Greensward Dynasty." About the same time the park began to go downhill rapidly as the disappearance of many varieties of trees, shrubs and vines give evidence. In the next decade or so general carelessness in maintenance and a casual acceptance of encroachments confirmed the bleak trend. With Parsons' resignation the landscape architect, to all intents and purposes, bowed out of the park scene.

Olmsted, Vaux and Parsons set and achieved certain standards for maintaining the park's landscape, managing to overcome many obstacles, including lack of funds. As Olmsted pointed out, neglect is not the worst disaster that can befall a park; far more formidable was the yearly threat of projects planned for the park by well-intentioned and not-so-well-intentioned promoters—trotting courses, world's fairs, churches, circuses, underground garages (proposed even before 1921), etc. When the park was menaced by a world's fair in 1881, public pressure forced the State Legislature to pass an act barring such exhibitions from the park. A bill permitting construction of a trotting speedway in the park went through the legislature in 1892; by staging demonstrations throughout the city, the public forced the act's repeal.

At the turn of the century Theodore Roosevelt's uncle came up with the not infrequent proposal of selling off some of the park to boost the city's finances. Actually, until the turn of the century the park was spared, except for the Menagerie at the Arsenal and the Metropolitan Museum of Art, both of which had come to be recognized as prime invaders. In 1881 the park even lost several structures, dating from pre-park days, as a result of fire. Yet the commercialization of Central Park was and still is a continuing threat.

If the nineteenth century had to a large degree successfully held off invasion, the twentieth cannot make the same boast. The new era has seen three forces emerge—the automobile, active recreation and the philanthropy of good works—and three have found their way onto the greensward.

Olmsted and Vaux, no more than the rest of their contemporaries, could hardly have foreseen the automobile, that wonderful ruthless instrument of man, let alone prepare for the throughways and garages it entailed. By the early 1890's a few cars had coughed their way into the city; the first automobile race in New York took place on May 30, 1896. By the summer of 1899, Central Park was the only one of the city's parks to bar automobiles. Chafing at this restriction, the Automobile Club of American sent intrepid car drivers into the park to gain arrest and martyrdom. The club won its cause on November 27, 1899, when Permit No. 1 was granted to a Mr. Curtis O. Brady "to enter upon and pass over the drives of Central Park with his electric automobile runabout," with the warning "to exercise the greatest care to avoid frightening horses. . . ." The speed limit was set at seven miles per hour (eight miles per hour was the ordinary city limit, fifteen on country roads) to be decreased to three and one-half miles per hour when the car approached a carriage or equestrian. The Greensward plan had deliberately curved the drives to prevent their being used by rapid traffic. To restrict drive use further, no entrances had been provided at

Sixth and Seventh avenues at the park's southern limit on 59th Street. A temporary access road was cut at Seventh Avenue around 1900; it was made permanent in 1905. The Sixth Avenue entrance was not cut through until 1924. Park officials complained in 1906 that the drives were being ruined by the cars. Particularly destructive were the heavy chains the early cars used in wet weather to prevent skidding. By 1912 asphalt replaced gravel on the drives. Several of the old carriage "resting places" or "road stops" eventually were converted to "parking lots." By 1920 the automobile had taken over the park, and the drives became throughways.

Active recreation requiring permanent installations was the second force of change. Originally *recreation* was thought of in terms of refreshing oneself with food and drink. The meaning then broadened to include forms of quiet distraction such as leisurely strolling; in Olmsted and Vaux's day *recreation* was still used in this sense and meant as applied to the park, pleasure found in viewing a landscape as opposed to harassment by city bustle and noise. The two men frequently turned to the word *tranquilize*, to describe the response they wanted the park to elicit; currently, of course, the word is associated with a pill. Sports years ago had nothing to do with "recreation."

As the park's aim and usage were to be completely democratic, no particular group was to be catered to. Among the first to step forward with special requests were athletic groups. The most demanding, in Olmsted and Vaux's eyes, were the ballplayers, whom they felt were incapable of grasping the concept of democracy in a park.

> *It seems difficult for them to realize that the large open surface of turf that, to the cultivated taste is among the most attractive features of the Park, can have any other use than that of a playground* [they lamented in 1865], *and nothing is more certain than that the beauty of these lawns would*

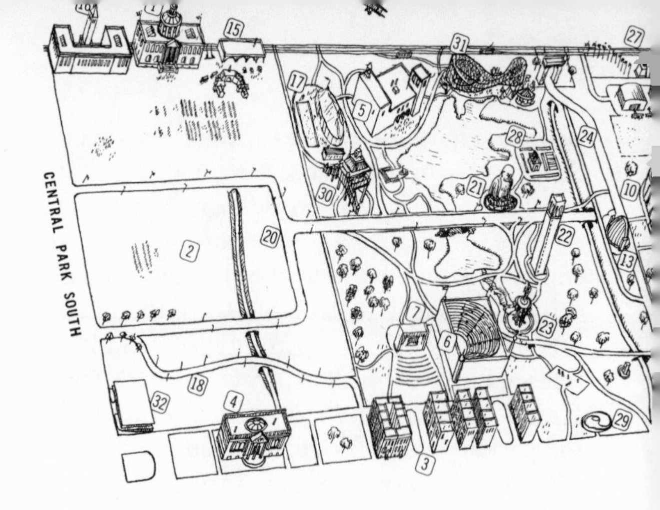

"IMPROVEMENTS" SUGGESTED FOR CENTRAL PARK SINCE 1900

Sketch by Ken Fitzgerald, based on information supplied by Alan Becker

1. Exposition Building, 1903.
2. Drill ground, 1904.
3. Selling off lower park for building lots, 1904; proposed for west side of Fifth Avenue by Mayor La Guardia in 1930's.
4. Building for National Academy of Design, 1909.
5. Opera House, 1910.
6. Outdoor theatre seating 50,000, 1911; opera amphitheatre proposed 1933.
7. Marionette theatre, 1912; proposed again 1964 and 1965.
8. Relocation of Central Park West streetcar tracks, 1917.
9. Trenches in North Meadow as war display, 1918.
10. Large stadium, 1919.
11. Airplane field, 1919.
12. Sunken oriental garden, Memorial Hall for war trophies and sports amphitheatre, 1920.
13. Music stand and road connecting drives to be called Mitchel Memorial, 1920.
14. Underground parking lot for 30,000 cars, 1921; proposed many times since.

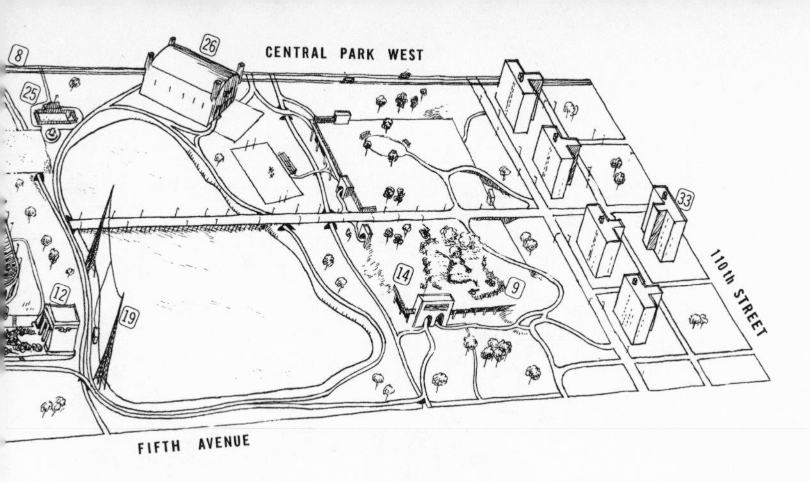

Suggested "Improvements" to Central Park since 1900 as seen by Ken Fitzgerald. Based on information gathered by Alan Becker.
Greensward Foundation.

15. Police garage, 1921.
16. Music and Art Center, 1922.
17. Swimming pool, circus and running track, 1923.
18. Filling in of Pond for new driveway, 1923.
19. Radio towers for city radio station, 1923.
20. Central roadway to relieve city's traffic congestion, 1923.
21. Statue of Buddha, 1925.
22. Carillon tower, 1925.
23. Fountain of the Seasons, 1929.
24. Promenade connecting Metropolitan and Natural History Museums, 1930.
25. Recreation building and swimming pool, 1935.
26. Armory and stables, 1940.
27. Plaza of South America, 8 acres, 1941.
28. Recreation Center for the Elderly, 1955.
29. Garden for the Blind, 1955.
30. El Station as monument to Elevated Railroad, 1955.
31. Amusement Center, 1955.
32. Huntington Hartford Outdoor Café, 1960.
33. Housing Project, 106th to 110th Streets, 1964.

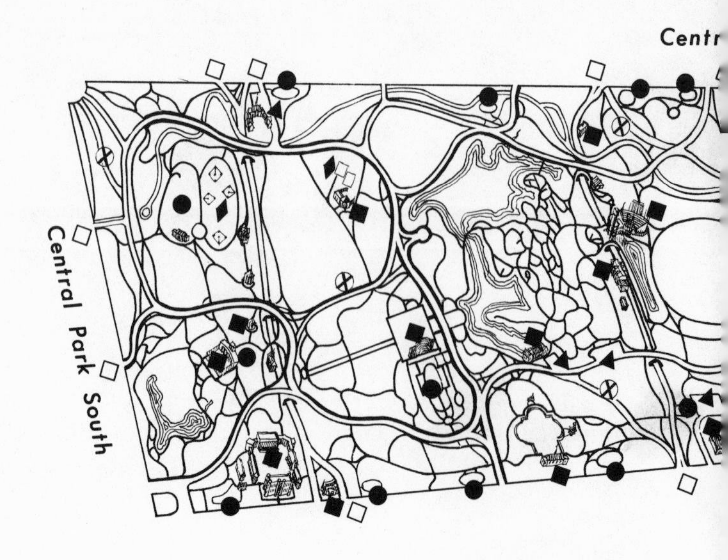

MAJOR IMPROVEMENTS IN CENTRAL PARK SINCE 1900

Sketch by Ken Fitzgerald

Key:

- ■ Building
- ● Playground
- ◆ Sports field, fenced and unfenced
- □ Access to drive and transverse roads
- ⊗ Discontinued drive
- ▲ New or enlarged parking space

Note: Map does not include new foot or bicycle paths, gardens, memorials, flagpoles, statuary or razed buildings, filling in of bodies of water, stone and concrete embankments, concrete benches, galvanized-iron lampposts and extensive asphalting.

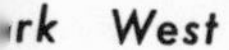

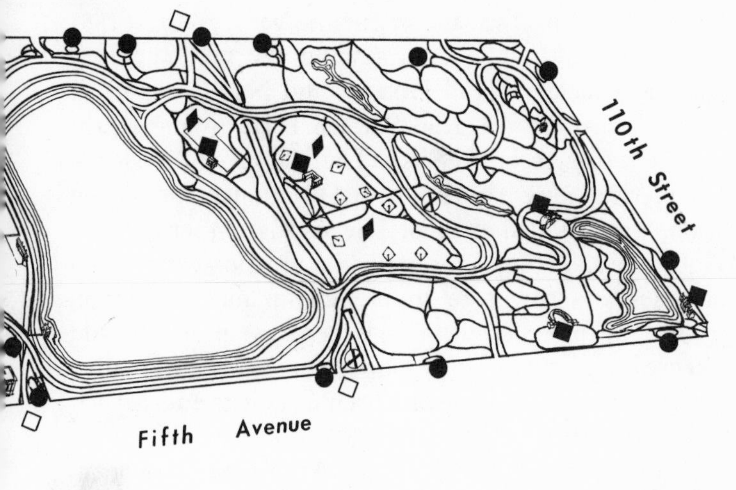

Improvements since 1900. Map by Ken Fitzgerald.
Greensward Foundation.

soon be lost, and that they would be rendered disagreeable objects, if these games were to be constantly played upon them. . . . It would tend to depreciate the attractions of the Park to the far greater number who visit it for the refined pleasures that its landscape affords to those who are sensitive to natural beauties. . . . And this use is not to be diminished to accommodate sports, of themselves innocent and worthy of encouragement, but participated in by comparatively few persons.

Sports had their place in the park but were limited to a great extent to schoolchildren and then only on certain days of the week and only on a few specified lawns such as the Ball Ground (called the Play Ground in the Greensward plan), now part of Heckscher Playground. There were also several children's areas with wooden swings placed on lawns.

Now if the history of public recreation in America begins with Central Park, as the textbooks document, the concept moved rapidly away from the original definition. Wooden swings were joined by the sandlot for the very young (1885 in Boston), the children's playground in the contemporary sense (1892 at Chicago's Hull House), and New York's first equipment playground (1899 in Seward Park, owing to the efforts of the reformer Jacob Riis). The Playground Association of America, now the influential National Recreation Association, was founded in 1906. The association set up standards of acreage and equipment, trained recreation experts and prodded cities and towns to supply community recreation facilities. By the first decade of this century, park use and "active recreation" were synonymous; not long after 1910 Central Park had its first *permanent* tennis courts and *permanent* baseball diamonds.

The word *park* has also seen change. At one time primarily identified with the landscape, the term is now found in "ball park," "amusement park" and "industrial park." The final debasement came in the age of the automobile with *parking lot* and *to park*, which have nothing remotely to do with trees, shrubs and lawn. In contrast the word *garden* has remained relatively unsullied.

With the 1920's a third force for change had joined the automobile and equipment recreation, a phenomenon peculiar to Central Park: the philanthropist with the "*useful* gift." The park's defenders had always had to battle aggressive donors, but evidently it was easier to keep out monuments than it was to bar good works. The Heckscher Playground of 1925 took over seventeen acres of what had been heretofore called simply "The Ball Ground." Fences were put up and an extensive concrete wading pool installed. (The large asphalt apron dates from 1936.) Bitterly attacked at the time, the donor nonetheless *forced* his way onto the greensward and firmly attached his name to the "gift." This was the first "personal memorial" in the park.

One of the least successful bits of sculpture in the park, it might be noted, forms part of the Heckscher Playground—the Sophie Loeb Memorial. Caricatures of Tenniel's illustrations for *Alice in Wonderland* provide the subject. The tone of the inscriptions matches the quality of the sculpture: "Her greatest wealth was her heart of gold"; "May I never fail a friend nor fight a foe but fairly."

All three forces, not evil in themselves but only in their misapplication within a landscaped park must be recognized to grasp what has taken place in Central Park in more recent times. Contributing to change was yet another force, more subtle but equally pervasive: the neglect or dismissal of the past, so much part of the frame of reference of modern art. Admittedly this last, although still very much present, is a passing fashion and happily there are signs of progress, notably in the growing awareness of America's artistic heritage. The modernist's emphasis on functionalism, so current at one time, was translated in park terms to emphasize "active use" or "entertainment" to the exclusion of the park as a work of art; this is less true today. Even architects now see that there is a higher dimension than a simplistic acceptance of "use."

A little-known report on the park, made in 1927 by the landscape architect, Hermann W. Merkel, attempted to meet the challenge presented by recreation. In so doing, the report and Mr. Merkel inadvertently opened the door to a variety of "improvements," the very ones, in fact that Olmsted and Vaux had always protested. While admitting that the Heckscher Playground and tennis courts (Samuel Parsons had protested these last) were "encroachments" and "an inharmonious element," with "their incongruous fences and apparatus . . ." Merkel suggested that eight children's playgrounds be placed at park entrances. At the same time he warned that "in setting aside these spots, the ultimate concession has been made"—to the pressure of recreation experts. "The ultimate concession" in marginal playgrounds now numbers nineteen! It was also Merkel who suggested that anchored concrete benches (first installed in 1928) should replace the old, movable cast-iron ones. Formerly these concrete benches were set on the paths; now they are set on concrete aprons off the paths. Pointing to the sorry condition of the Cave on the western edge of the Ramble, he advised that if it was not cleaned it would be better walled up. It was walled up, and another touch of Olmsted and Vaux disappeared.

By far the greater part of Merkel's report was devoted to planting. While he found the park's condition as "fairly good," he noted the appalling deterioration; evidently, after Parsons left in 1911, neglect took on disastrous proportions. ". . . All but three or four of the varieties of evergreens," wrote Merkel, "have to all intents and purposes disappeared from the park, and very many of the deciduous ones." The "Winter Drive" no longer existed, and the several weeping varieties of beech, birch, larch and linden had gone, as well as the one camperdown elm. (Prospect Park, whose planting offers a useful comparison, can still boast of its camperdown elm.) It was not so much the lack of good topsoil that did the damage as the hard packing of the existing soil. This condition resulted from overuse, which only ever-present control and attention could prevent.

Merkel pointed out that only adequate policing and maintenance could protect the landscape. The solution, he thought, would be a special park police, a force made up of men trained in park work, such as the group Olmsted once had under his control and that still exist in other cities. As for maintenance he asked that the park have its own superintendent with seven or eight foremen, each with a crew of gardeners and assistant gardeners; each foreman and crew were to be *permanently* assigned to seven or eight sections of park land. Although he gave no figure for the existing staff, he insisted that it be doubled. (The authors have been unable to trace the appendix of the report devoted to the maintenance staff and its organization.) One suggestion he made to rescue the greensward was promptly carried out. Up to then watering had been done by portable hose connected with hydrants, which Olmsted and Vaux had placed along the drives and spotted through the rest of the park. At a cost of $1,000,000 a system of sprinkler irrigation, made up of water lines and sprinkler heads, was placed below ground. One of the great sights of the park in the early 1930's was the sea of white spray on the lawns during the summer.

Other changes outlined by Merkel would have followed had not the Panic of 1929 struck the city. The breakdown in the park became total as the unemployed were allowed to have sheds in the more secluded hollows and even out on open ground—on the dried bed of the Old Reservoir emptied in 1929. Misery found refuge in the park; the "Hoovervilles," as they were known, presented a fantastic scene reminiscent of the squatter colonies of the 1850's. In 1934, with the coming of Mayor La Guardia to City Hall, work in the park began

"Hooverville" in Central Park, 1930–1931. The site is the dried bed of the old Receiving Reservoir, now the Great Lawn. The twin towers of the Eldorado rise off Central Park West.

Museum of the City of New York.

again. One of the first steps was the reorganization of the Park Department. A single commissioner replaced the five-member board. Robert Moses was named commissioner, a title he held until 1960 when he was succeeded by the late Newbold Morris, in office until the beginning of 1966. The Merkel report was dusted off to serve as a plan of action. As noted above, the marginal playgrounds were put in and the Cave blocked off. In addition the Zoo, which Merkel had asked be housed in one building, was enlarged and placed in a half-dozen brick structures. The west arm of the Lake, which the landscape man had considered a nuisance, was filled in; this apparently initiated a policy of neglecting bodies of water throughout the park, for silting has gone on in the Lake, the Loch has dwindled to nothing and two acres were lost to the Pond with the installation of the Wollman Skating Rink. New walks that Merkel had advised for some of the trampled paths, and that judiciously, were spread indiscriminately.

Merkel's injunction of proper upkeep for the old park structures was disregarded wholesale. Rustic shelters and arbors were allowed to deteriorate and, if not blown down, were razed as dangerous. The report's recommendations on planting and its maintenance met with complete indifference. The water lines, installed in 1928, were neglected to the extent that they no longer exist. The staff of gardeners and assistant gardeners, inadequate in 1927, was reduced, and today it is smaller than ever. The pastoral park was dismissed altogether, symbolized by the removal of the sheep from the Sheep Meadow in 1934. The Park Department no longer had an official landscape architect; by inadvertence the position was omitted from the 1936 charter and never reinstated. Landscape architecture, when needed, was given out on contract and the work done under the supervision of the department's engineer or architect.

The most serious invasion of the park took the form of gifts, several of which were personal memorials partly financed by the city. The more prominent of the gifts have been the Wollman Skating Rink in 1950, the Hans Christian Andersen statue in 1956, the Alice-in-Wonderland group in 1959, the Delacorte (Shakespeare) Theatre in 1963 and the disastrous Loula D. Lasker Pool-Rink. Little wonder that the park has won the name of "Central Park Memorial Cemetery." The attitude of an administration that permitted these contraventions to the Olmsted and Vaux ideal is in sharp contrast to the common sense and high purpose of the Londoners in charge of Hyde Park. "Well, some suggestion for exploiting Hyde Park is put forward nearly every week," remarked one of the park's guardians recently, "and the reason why it stays unspoilt is because people damn well see that it stays so!"

Much of the permanent damage to the park has taken place since the war, in the very decades that the nation has presumably known an "artistic explosion." For all today's self-consciousness about the importance of "ART," the particular work of art called Central Park has been forgotten. Some have speculated that it was misnamed in the 1850's. Had it been called, for example, "The New York Public Gardens" there would have been no desecration. The sheep would still be on the Sheep Meadow and the Swanboats on the pond (there until 1924), much as they still are in the Boston Public Gardens. The word "garden," like the flaming sword at the Garden of Eden, might have protected the greensward.

A renewed effort to save the park has sprung, as so often happens in human affairs, from a surprising source. With the 1950's, America, and it is true of other nations, found itself preoccupied with the destruction of its visible heritage. In New York the awareness was driven home by the erosion of classical Park Avenue, once a proud residential thoroughfare.

More shocking was the destruction of Pennsylvania Station. A temporary Landmarks Preservation Commission, launched by Mayor Robert F. Wagner in 1962, was made permanent three years later. As far as Central Park was concerned a turning point was reached in June, 1965, when the National Park Service of the Department of the Interior declared it a National Historic Landmark. More important, parks and recreation became an issue in the mayoralty campaign of that year when John V. Lindsay issued a white paper on "Parks and Playgrounds." A special section of the paper dealt with Central Park and Prospect Park. Mayor Lindsay lamented the fact that the parks had not been placed under the jurisdiction of the Landmarks Preservation Commission as demanded in 1964 by Paul O'Dwyer, then a councilman. The white paper denounced another personal memorial, a café proposed for the southeast corner of Fifth Avenue and 59th Street and suggested *temporary* refreshment kiosks throughout the park; it met Councilman O'Dwyer's demand by proposing the appointment of a Curator of Central Park whose chief duty would be to assemble all necessary material with a view to achieving "exact reconstructions made of certain of the now missing original elements, in the same accurate manner that Colonial Williamsburg has been brought to life." On attaining office Mayor Lindsay appointed Thomas P. F. Hoving, Curator of the Cloisters, Commissioner of Parks; the naming of a curator both of Central and Prospect parks followed. The commissioner swiftly carried out the white paper proposal of turning down the "gift" of the café. Then, in a surprise move, he barred traffic in the park on Sundays.

Central Park, it must be remembered, while by far the most important single park, forms only 840 acres out of a total of 14,500 acres, readily accessible, in the park system. The commissioner's domain ranges from small vest-pocket parks to Shea Stadium and includes cultural and scientific institutions subsidized by the city. Yet this vast domain is starved for funds. The Department of Parks has always been a municipal stepchild and, within the department, the planting and landscaping divisions have been the departmental stepchildren since 1910.

But the steps taken and promised will mean nothing without essential policing and maintenance. The question of policing—and that extends to the prevention of vandalism—is nothing new in the park's history. Merkel had to consider it, as did others before him. "Here we touch a fact of more value to social science than any other in the history of the park . . ." Olmsted wrote in 1870, and even then he was talking from experience. "The difficulty of preventing ruffianism and disorder in a park to be frequented indiscriminately by such a population as that of New York, was from the first regarded as the greatest of all those which the Commission had to meet and the means of overcoming it cost more study than all other things." From 1936 until 1942, the Police Commissioner, acting on the request of the Park Department, deputized Park Supervisors and a few of the other park employees, empowering them to issue summonses for violations of park regulations. In a modified form, policing by park employees continued until 1947 but was not found very satisfactory. What is obviously required today is additional training of the police assigned to the park, the kind of training that men on the force obtain when given such special duties as handling civil disturbances and dealing with youngsters. Use might be made of such instruments as the Police Athletic League. Some knowledge of the park's history and of planting would be helpful. New Yorkers must be made to realize that the park is their very own and that, in damaging it, they damage their own property. Aiding the police should be auxiliaries, similar to school-crossing guards or meter maids who might be called "park maids."

Their presence would, in addition, help counteract the obsessive fear of crime in the park. Actually crime has not changed much over the years. While in 1872 there were 37 arrests for felony, in 1965 there were, it is true, 104 felony complaints and arrests; but if there are more felonies today, drunkenness is not the nuisance it was in 1872, accounting for 199 arrests. The safest precinct in the city is the 74th, devoted to Prospect Park; the next safest is the Central Park Precinct, which is staffed at the peak season by 165 patrolmen, 25 mounted police and 10 scooter police, the last force to be considerably enlarged. Fear of crime in the park is based not on fact but on exaggeration. Crime is a citywide problem, but incidents that take place in the sylvan setting somehow strike the public as much more ominous than those happening on a city street. If there is a so-called "crime wave" in the park, planting is removed for greater visibility, yet if a "crime wave" strikes Madison Avenue no buildings are blown up. A rehabilitation program for the park's planting, begun in 1957 and not yet completed, has been publicized as removing planting for crime prevention. Little or no mention has been made of beautification of the landscape.

Actually the best crime deterrent in the park is first-class maintenance. Damaged shrubbery, broken glass, neglected turf, silted waters, widespread erosion—these and other evidences of neglect invite lawlessness. And there must be an end to what has the unfortunate, if justifiable name of "official vandalism" namely concrete curbing, concrete benches and galvanized-iron lampposts; there are alternatives. In seeking the solution for maintenance it is worth accepting Hermann W. Merkel's proposal of a superintendent for the park, with a staff of nine foremen (seven of them for seven sections, with two extra to fill in for vacations, etc.), backed by thirty trained gardeners and thirty assistant gardeners, plus a roving force of pruners and climbers, amounting roughly to ninety men altogether. They would form a separately administered staff, permanently in the park, even permanently assigned to sections. To underscore the difficulties under which the present horticulturist's staff operates, it should be noted that the fall 1965 program for new planting was put off because of the drought. This made for a double program in the spring of 1966; at the same time, due to the drought, the new planting could not be watered. Very few realize what the Borough Horticulturist is up against. It is almost essential, also, to provide a new system of water lines. What should be aimed for in the entire park is the standard now attained in a few high-maintenance areas; the grounds at the Arsenal or Park Department headquarters offer the best example.

New Yorkers must learn the hard way, as they have in the preservation of landmarks. Commissioner Hoving was to point out on more than one occasion that the beginning of any program for the park lies with a thorough study of the reports of Olmsted and Vaux. Not only will such a study reveal that the problems are generations old but also, and this is more important, that Central Park is, in truth, a garden, a work of art. In a picturesque composition such as a landscaped park the position of every grove, outcrop of rock, line of a walk and body of water has been thought out in terms of design. Central Park is no different from a large classical mural in fresco, a vast historical canvas or a traditional relief teeming with figures. A Greek relief is not cleaned by scouring it with steel brushes, nor should change be made in a park without being carefully considered in the terms of the original design. No one would consider tampering with a Beethoven symphony, although the orchestra's size, not to mention variety of instruments, has changed since his day. Nor would anyone dare to repaint a portion of "Washington Crossing the Delaware." In much the same way nothing must be altered in the composition called Central Park.

It should not be forgotten that a city, like a nation, is judged by the care it lavishes on its monuments, and the importance of this rule grows more obvious every day. Let those who neglect or maim the monument called Central Park beware. When the public relations man has passed on, when the self-promotion of the living has stopped, history shows no mercy in its condemnation, any more than it stints in its praise.

View in Central Park: Bow Bridge, Island and Ramble in the distance.

Valentine's Manual, 1861

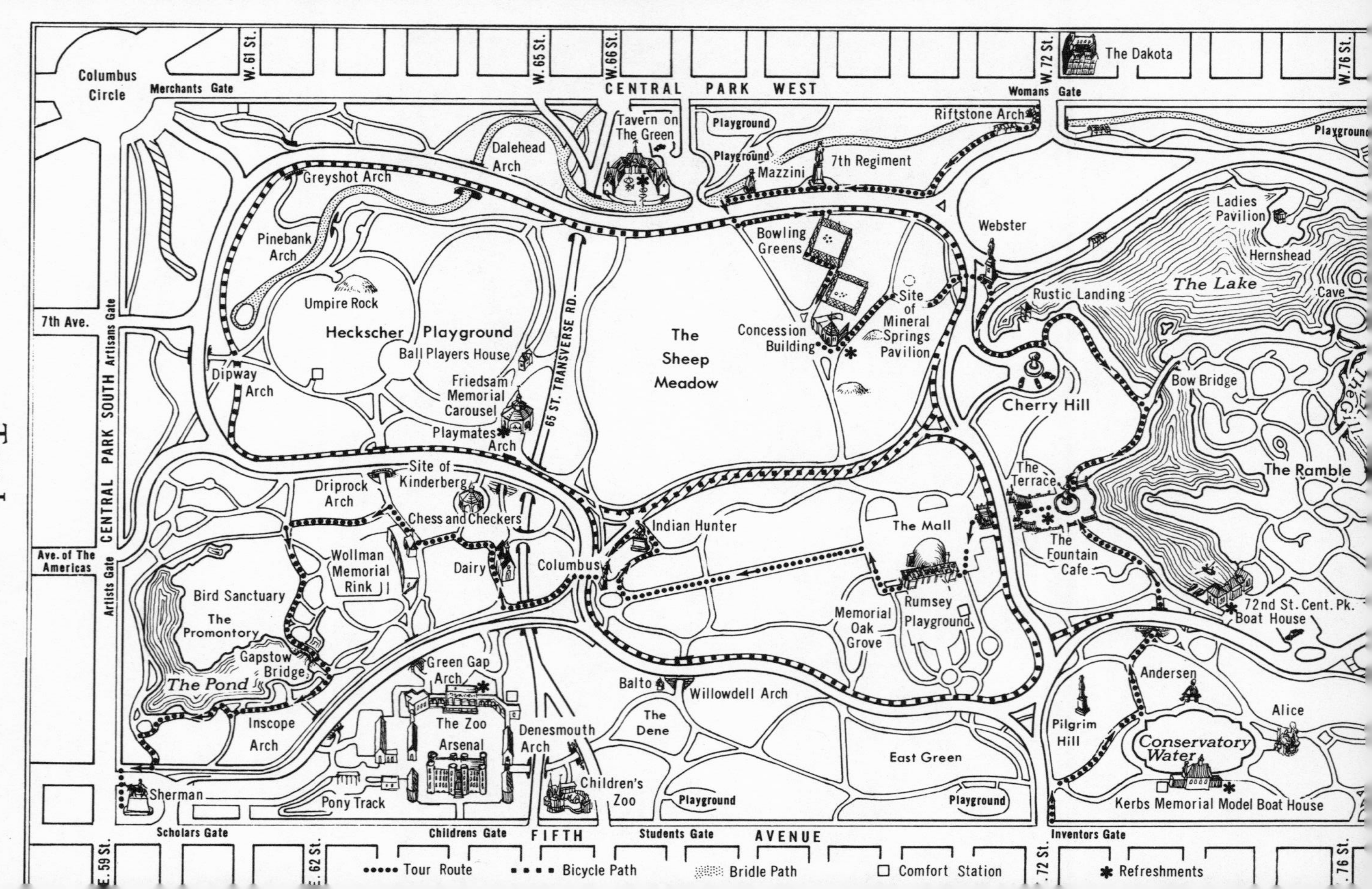
CENTRAL PARK WEST
CENTRAL PARK SOUTH
FIFTH AVENUE
W. 61 St.
W. 65 St.
W. 66 St.
W. 72 St.
W. 76 St.
E. 59 St.
E. 62 St.
E. 72 St.
E. 76 St.
Columbus Circle
Merchants Gate
Womans Gate
Artisans Gate
Artists Gate
Scholars Gate
Childrens Gate
Students Gate
Inventors Gate
7th Ave.
Ave. of The Americas
The Dakota
Tavern on The Green
Playground
Riftstone Arch
7th Regiment
Mazzini
Dalehead Arch
Greyshot Arch
Pinebank Arch
Umpire Rock
Heckscher Playground
Ball Players House
Friedsam Memorial Carousel
Playmates Arch
65 ST. TRANSVERSE RD.
Dipway Arch
The Sheep Meadow
Bowling Greens
Concession Building
Site of Mineral Springs Pavilion
Webster
Ladies Pavilion
Hernshead
The Lake
Cave
Rustic Landing
Bow Bridge
The Gill
Cherry Hill
The Ramble
The Terrace
The Fountain Cafe
72nd St. Cent. Pk. Boat House
Site of Kinderberg
Driprock Arch
Chess and Checkers
Indian Hunter
The Mall
Wollman Memorial Rink
Dairy
Columbus
Rumsey Playground
Memorial Oak Grove
Bird Sanctuary
The Promontory
Gapstow Bridge
The Pond
Green Gap Arch
Balto
Willowdell Arch
Andersen
Alice
Pilgrim Hill
Conservatory Water
Inscope Arch
The Zoo
Arsenal
Denesmouth Arch
The Dene
East Green
Children's Zoo
Sherman
Pony Track
Kerbs Memorial Model Boat House
Tour Route
Bicycle Path
Bridle Path
Comfort Station
Refreshments

Tour I

II

WALKING TOUR OF THE SOUTHERN SECTION

Transportation: For Central Park West and 72nd Street: 72nd Street Stations of the IND and West Side IRT Subways; Eighth Avenue Bus Line

This tour of the Southern or Lower Section of the park has two starting points: one at Central Park West and 72nd Street; the other at Fifth Avenue and 72nd Street. From either side, west or east, the tour leads to the Terrace and continues south as one tour, ending at 59th Street and Fifth Avenue. The East Side alternate is described after the West Side approach.

The tour begins at the Womens Gate, across from the gabled Dakota, one of the earliest and most elegant of New York's apartment houses, built in 1881 on the design of Henry Janeway Hardenbergh, later architect of the Hotel Plaza. The Dakota's residents were the first apartment dwellers to get a sweeping park view from the West Side. The sidewalk of Central Park West bordering the park is lined with a single row of pin oaks, among the hardier trees to flourish in the city. Olmsted and Vaux set great importance on this tree-lined border, intending it as a leafy screen to keep the approaching city out of view from the park. Up to the turn of the century, this screen worked to a fair degree, but with the coming of the big apartment houses and skyscrapers the city rose far above the tree line and presented an entirely new skyline, which, as seen from the park, is one of the great city spectacles.

Although the Womens Gate bears no inscription, it has been called that since 1862 when the park's original eighteen gates were named: Artisans, Artists, Merchants, Scholars, Cultivators (now Farmers), Warriors, Mariners, Engineers, Hunters, Woodman's, Explorers (now Pioneers), Inventors, Foreigners (changed to Strangers, possibly because the city's enormous immigrant population took umbrage), Boys, Girls, Childrens, Womens and All Saints (changed to Prophets and then back again). (For location of these gates see end map.) Under the aegis of the Central Park Association, now the Park Association of New York City, formed to fight encroachments on the park, the gates were formally dedicated in 1926, a prominent citizen lending his sponsorship to each gate. Despite this ceremony the gates must soon have faded from public notice, for to date only three of the original ones have been inscribed—Mariners, Inventors and Engineers.

While the park was being built, each gate had a gatehouse and a gatekeeper who saw to it that visitors entered the park only at the appointed hours of opening. In the 1860's the park was open from 7 A.M. to 8 P.M. during the winter months (except when night ice skating postponed the closing until midnight), from 5 A.M. to 11 P.M. during the hot summer months, and from 6 A.M. to 9 P.M. the rest of the year. The Park Commissioners thought that the park unquestionably should be closed at night: "The park will be useless for any good purpose, after dusk, for . . . the public cannot be secured safe transit through large open spaces of ground after nightfall." Olmsted, who felt strongly about this matter, later vigorously protested against the installation of gas lights, claiming they could not adequately protect the public from danger. Today the park is officially closed from midnight until dawn, and the police do their best to see that this ruling is enforced.

The promenader takes the path to the south of the drive, passing a green wall of *Euonymus kiautschovica*, barberry (*Berberis juliana*) and privet (*Ligustrum vulgare*). The *Euonymus* was placed in the city's parks about a decade ago by Cornelius O'Shea, Horticulturist of the Borough of Manhattan, and it is found chiefly at park entrances. A hardy plant, it is a handsome one thanks to its shiny dark green leaf. The spiky barberry serves to discourage any exploring of the hedge. As the path turns and drops, the promenader enters a wooden arbor of Chinese wisteria (*Wisteria sinensis*), which greets the spring with large violet flowers. This rustic arbor forms a covered gate, a welcoming entrance, and is one of many rustic embellishments that used to be found in the park. Arbors, summerhouses and benches–some of ingenious design–were scattered about, providing shaded retreats. There are left only three vine-covered arbors as well as the vine-covered Pergola behind the Bandshell on the Mall. Drinking fountains and litter baskets were also formerly rustic and were surely more pleasing to the eye than the concrete cubes and wire baskets encountered along the way.

A short distance beyond the arbor the promenader can abandon the walk to go down to the edge of the bridle path on the right and look back. He will be delighted to discover that he has, on entering the park, crossed a bridge so skillfully designed and landscaped that he was unaware of being over a bridle path. This is a typical Olmsted and Vaux touch–part of the careful separation of traffic that is so much part of their design. The rustic element is maintained in the construction of the bridge by the use of little mortar and big blocks of Manhattan schist, probably excavated from the bridle-path cut. The architects believed that structures in a picturesque landscape should be "natural"; the use of thick mortar and brick or smaller stones in the bridge would have been "unnatural." All of the park's original bridges, the work of Calvert Vaux, were of different design and most have names, identified on the end sheet maps. This bridge is the Riftstone Arch.

Returning to the path, the promenader continues south. At this point the path sinks lower than the drive to the left, obtaining a distinct separation from the drive, a separation underscored by planting. On the right is the standard park lamppost, designed in 1907 by Henry Bacon, architect of the Lincoln Memorial in Washington. The lamppost heads are being replaced by hapless ones of modern design during the completion of a $2,500,000 program to improve Central Park lighting; the program, begun in 1958, has left the original attractive heads in the neighborhood of the Zoo and in several other highly frequented spots. On the lamppost, the promenader will notice a small plaque with the number 7105, the first two digits indicating that it stands on the parallel of 71st Street. All park lampposts bear this street-designating plaque. Beyond the post, also on the right, are three trees with orange bark; they are Osage oranges (*Maclura pomifera*), a tree which captures children's fancy because of its green fruit, four to five inches in diameter. In the fall the heavy fruit sometimes crashes down, to the annoyance of New Yorkers who, unaccustomed to the vagaries of nature, send in complaints to the Park Department. As the path approaches the drive there is to be seen on the left a species of tree with strange clusters of tangled twigs, "witches' broom," a fungus in the branches; the tree is the common hackberry (*Celtis occidentalis*). At hand is an example of the concrete bench that has become standard; it was first introduced in 1928. Found, as it is, in quantity throughout the park, it heads the list of visual offenses.

Here at the drive there used to be arbors on both sides of the crossing as if to compensate for the absence of a bridge. The tour continues south, west of the drive, to the Civil War Memorial of the Seventh Regiment by John Quincy Adams Ward. A Union soldier leaning on his rifle, it brings to mind similar statues found on greens and squares in towns throughout the North and Midwest; no other monument evokes the sadness of the fratricidal war quite so sharply. Ward, one of America's great sculptors, treated the figure in the classical manner—the best ancient example being the stele relief of an Athenian soldier leaning on his spear, mourning those lost at Marathon.

From the start Olmsted, Vaux and the Park Commissioners had to battle the compulsion of New Yorkers to turn the greensward into a memorial ground, and it is a continuing battle. The issue, then as always, was controversial and led the commissioners in 1867 to define their position as follows:

> *The Commissioners of the Park have been thus guarded in dealing with this subject [Seventh Regiment Monument] because they have deemed the Park not an appropriate place for sepulchral memorials; it is for recreation and pleasure; its especial aim and object is, by all justifiable means, to dispel from the mind of the visitors, once within its enclosure, thoughts of business and memories calculated to sadden or oppress. It is a pleasure ground. The beautiful cemeteries in the vicinity of the city offer abundant opportunity to commemorate, by appropriate memorials, the virtues of those who are passing away from the strifes and distinctions of the cabinet or the field.*

Despite the commissioners' objections, Ward's statue was dedicated in 1870 with great ceremony.

It is an odd fact that nearly all the statues in the city's parks have a solemn, if not commemorative note. Not for New Yorkers of the last century, nor for others of the Victorian era, were the frivolous statues of the ancient or Renaissance world, the statues of the Shepherd's Calendar, of gods and goddesses, laughing satyrs or dancing nymphs. This was not so much a national rejection of public statuary redolent of paganism nor a barring of the Great God Pan and his crew at the frontier by immigration authorities but rather a nineteenth-century preoccupation with memorials in a park.

The Ward statue is outstanding, but that was not true of other statues offered to the park. To fend off donors the Park Commissioners adopted rules and standards for accepting sculpture. As an early park guide pointed out: "A second-rate statue is like a tolerable egg—it is not to be endured."

Notwithstanding the restrictions, statues continued to be erected. One objection to them was the need for maintenance, particularly in prevention of erosion around the base. At the Ward statue asphalt has solved the problem. Farther along the path there is another memorial, a bust of Giuseppe Mazzini, 1805-1872, by G. Turini. Mazzini, the great Italian republican and anticlerical who laid the foundation for the unification of Italy, was a hero to Americans in the last century. The monument was dedicated by William Cullen Bryant on May 29, 1878. One result of the excitement of the occasion was that the eighty-four-year-old poet, who had pressed so hard for the creation of a Central Park, suffered an accident and died not long after, on June twelfth, at his home in Roslyn, Long Island.

Beyond the Mazzini Monument is the Tavern-on-the-Green, a restaurant surrounded by parked cars. For that reason and because of the view of the lot afforded by the picture windows of the main dining room, as well as the cars parked on the bridle path in front of the terrace on summer evenings, the restaurant is sometimes referred to as "Tavern-on-the-Parking Lot." Originally this building was the Sheepfold, designed by Jacob Wrey Mould to house the sheep, which grazed on the Green or Sheep Meadow opposite, and their resident shepherd. Twice a day the shepherd used to hold up traffic on the drive and herd his flock across. When a reforming administration came to power in 1934, they claimed that the Southdown sheep were inbred and producing malformed progeny and exiled the flock to Prospect Park from where they were banished not long after.

The history of the Sheepfold and its adjacent lands illustrates the pattern of encroachment inflicted on the park. The Sheepfold was built at the order of the infamous "Tweed Ring," which mismanaged park affairs in 1870-71. Olmsted

Sheep on the Sheep Meadow, one of the sights of the Park prior to 1934. *New York Junior League.*

protested its siting, since it could be reached directly only by walking across the bridle path, and ridiculed the plan of the Tweed commissioners to hang portraits of sheep and specimens of wool in pavilions for visitors. When the "Tweed Ring" was ousted from power in 1871 Olmsted and Vaux were again offered the appointment of Landscape Architects; they accepted with the proviso that no building could be erected in the park without their approval of the plans.

In 1905, a temporary access road at 66th Street, to the rear of the Sheepfold, was made permanent for the convenience of equestrians and carriage drivers. When the building was transformed into a restaurant in 1934, it was provided with a parking lot and a new entrance on 67th Street; the 66th Street access became a service entrance. Suddenly, in 1956, while the restaurant was being renovated, a bulldozer one day appeared to plow up land for an additional parking lot, permission for which had been granted by the Park Department. An alert photographer nearby spotted the machine, called up friends and acquaintances and in no time, fifty angry mothers, children in tow, appeared and surrounded the bulldozer. Work stopped. Two days later the bulldozer reappeared, and again it was stopped, this time with the press in full attendance. "The Battle of the Tavern-on-the-Green" ended in partial victory for the public; a new playground was built.

Ill-conceived as the location of the Sheepfold might be, the presence of sheep in the meadow opposite fitted into the pastoral concept of the park's design. In Olmsted and Vaux's Greensward plan, this meadow was entitled "The Parade Ground," for one of the requirements of the design competition had been an area set aside for drilling. Fortunately once the park was built this use of it was deemed unsuitable. When the military, disregarding the ruling, insisted on drilling in the park several times the public and the Park Commissioners were outraged. A reminder that the pastoral is still very much present in the Sheep Meadow is the annual festival of folk dancing held in the late spring. Three thousand boys and girls, eleven- and twelve-year-old students from the public schools, gather here to perform eight dances, ending with one around fifty maypoles.

The promenader should cross the drive near the Mazzini Monument and take the path due north past a grove of small-leaved European lindens (*Tilia cordata*) on the right; a line of the familiar London planes (*Platanus acerifolia*) runs along the drive to the left. The park's London planes could more properly be called the "New York" planes, for they all come from the city nursery on Riker's Island where they are grown from cuttings of a disease-resistant strain; the ordinary London plane is prone to anthracnose, a nasty plant disease.

The bicycle path, located between the walk and the drive,

is an innovation of the mid-1930's. When cycling became a fad in the 1890's and cyclists had to compete for space on the drive with carriages and equestrians, an enterprising cyclist proposed that a "wheelway," consisting of two paths side by side, each ten feet wide, be built inside the park's perimeter. The question of "wheelways" was soon made obsolete by the arrival of the automobile. With asphalt instead of gravel on the drives and a forty-mile-per-hour speed limit Olmsted and Vaux's peaceful world of horse and carriage has completely disappeared.

The path continues to the bowling greens, one dating from the 1920's, the second from the 1930's, and goes right, skirting along the edge of the greens. Here, devotees of the ancient sport gather daily after the season opens. It is a very serious matter, this game, a fact brought home to any casual individual who obtains a bowling permit and tries to join the club-minded regulars. The path eventually comes on the Concession Building or Snack Bar, constructed in 1961, where service facilities and asphalt apron are larger than ever. Even were the present structure handsome, it is wholly out of place, for as the Greensward text pointed out:

> *Many elegant buildings may be appropriately erected for desirable purposes in a public park* [Olmsted and Vaux drastically changed their minds on this score], *but we conceive that all such architectural structures should be confessedly subservient to the main idea, and that nothing artificial should be obtruded in the view as an ultimatum of interest. The idea of the park itself should always be uppermost in the mind of the beholder.*

Built in a prominent position, the Concession Building ruins the vista of the north end of the Sheep Meadow, and, annoyingly, its siting entailed the paving of a network of new paths. Restrictions on lawn use once largely prevented the public from breaking new trails; if paths were trampled the ground was fenced off and reseeded. With the 1930's the lawns were thrown open, and the practice became to asphalt wherever earth is hammered to hardpan. Some points in the park, such as that just west of the Concession Building, take on the appearance of highway interchanges.

From the slight rise on the path just past the Concession Building, the view across the meadow is wonderful. Before the beholder lies the pastoral landscape—part meadow, part groves, seemingly thick woods and beyond, the city's great towers. From left to right the main ones are the Hotel Pierre with its steep green roof, the Sherry Netherland with its steeple, to the south, the low Plaza Hotel and behind the Plaza the shining spike of the Chrysler Building, the gargantuan Pan-Am building, so conveniently identified by a sign, the massive RCA slab with the globe of the weather station, the green-roofed Hampshire House and, last, the Essex House with its sign. To gain a sharper impression of the wonder the promenader should go down the slope to the left beyond the Concession Building and, at the bottom, turn to come back again. On reaching the top of the slope, he will see, in its fullest glory, the spectacle that overwhelmed John, a character in James Baldwin's best novel, *Go Tell It on the Mountain:*

> *Before him, then, the slope stretched upward, and above it the brilliant sky, and beyond it, cloudy and far away, he saw the skyline of New York. He did not know why, but there arose in him an exultation and a sense of power, and he ran up the hill like an engine, or a madman, willing to throw himself headlong into the city that glowed before him.*

The outcrop of rock on the slope invites inspection of local geology. Manhattan Island is floored by three kinds of rock: Inwood marble, some Fordham gneiss and, for the most part, Manhattan schist. This last is found throughout the park, recognizable by the presence of mica and its platelike quality, which makes it a poor building stone. The word *schist* comes from the French *schiste* for shale, and, in geological terms, it is a metamorphic rock, which means a rock produced by heat, pressure, and fluids. Manhattan schist was formed some 360,000,000 years ago in the Paleozoic era. (The amount of mica and more continuous foliation differentiate schist from gneiss; quartz and feldspar predominate in the latter as in Fordham gneiss, the floor rock of the Bronx.)

On top of the outcrop is a large glacial boulder or *erratic* left here 20,000 years ago in the course of the recession of the Laurentian Ice Sheet late in the Pleistocene epoch. These boulders–there are others on the south edge of the Sheep Meadow–were often carried considerable distances by the ice. On the surface of the schist outcrop can be seen rounded linear indentations or tracks as if giant fingers had pressed across the rock. The tracks, *striations* or *striae*, as they are called, run southeast-northwest and were made by rocks held in the ice sheet as it moved south and east, stopping just south of Manhattan. The erratics and the scratches are the main evidence of glaciers at work in Central Park; in Prospect Park, the evidence is in the form of moraines to be seen in the low knobs of the Long Meadow. But then, Long Island as a whole is one giant end moraine formed by the ice sheets.

The tour follows the path west around the Concession Building and at the fork turns right or north. To the left of the path, concealed in a grove, stood the old refreshment house, the wooden Mineral Springs Pavilion, designed by Vaux in the Gothic style. It was built in 1868 on the recommendation of prominent doctors who urged the Park Commissioners to include a place where "the waters" could be taken, thereby offering relief, supposedly, to those who suffered from gout, rheumatism, etc. Since one of the major purposes of the park was to provide a place of "healthful recreation," a spa seemed a logical idea. A mineral-waters firm, Schultz and Walker, erected the building at their own expense. Not long after, the

Mineral Springs Pavilion, designed by Calvert Vaux in 1868. Allowed to deteriorate, it was destroyed in 1960.

Museum of the City of New York.

Park Commissioners realized they had set a dangerous precedent by allowing a private concern to own a building in the park; the firm was reimbursed for the building's cost, ownership passing to the city. The Mineral Springs Pavilion achieved greatest vogue in the 1890's when, still under the management of Charles Schultz, it was referred to in the press as "Little Carlsbad" and offered a choice of thirty different types of mineral water to such prominent patrons as Jacob Ruppert, the brewer, and Chauncey Depew, the United States senator who headed the New York Central Railroad. (A decade earlier a natural spring in the park, near Central Park West in line with 82nd Street, gained fame for the nutritiousness of its waters. A Dr. Tanner claimed to have fasted forty days and forty nights, surviving on the spring water.)

The Mineral Springs Pavilion was the subject of great controversy within the Park Department. "The building was of considerable size," recalled Samuel Parsons, "and therefore, should be kept out of sight as far as the proper use of it will allow. All buildings, it may be said, from a landscape architect's point of view, are hardly tolerable in a park. The artistic value of the territory would be greater without them. If, however, they must be tolerated, then by all means the landscape architect should try to shut them out as much as he can. Frequently this does not suit the lessee. . . ." It did not suit Mr. Schultz, and the Park Commissioners allowed a stand of Norway spruce sheltering the building to be chopped down in 1883. Defending the trees, Parsons lost his job as Superintendent of Planting, but, thanks to Mayor William R. Grace, he eventually won the issue, becoming Superintendent of Parks and replanting the area. The Mineral Springs Pavilion remained standing until 1960. Due to conscious neglect, it fell into disrepair and was torn down to be replaced by the new Concession Building.

Just before the path begins to drop to the drive below, the promenader will see on the right an elm growing out of a crevice in a rock—a prime example of the struggle in nature, emphasized in the picturesque landscape tradition. The glacial grooves of this outcrop are wider than those in the outcrop discussed previously, but it will be noticed that they are oriented in the same southeast-northwest direction. Some of the park's schist has gold-bearing quartz but hardly enough to invite mining. Not a few times, iron pyrites or fool's gold embedded in the quartz has been mistaken for the precious metal and invited excitement.

Beyond to the left, from spring to fall, the ground is carpeted with Japanese knotweed (*Polygonum cuspidatum*) found throughout the park. Introduced not long ago into this country, this hardy plant has become a useful weed, although in quantity it is a nuisance.

Sleighing in the mid-1880's near the Webster statue. The Dakota apartment house can be glimpsed to the left of the statue. From *Harper's Weekly.* *The New York Times.*

Rustic shelter at a boat landing and rock outcrop, c. 1860, and in 1966. The original shelter was more substantial with its thatched roof, and soil, once on the rock, has long since eroded. See the engraving opposite title page. *New-York Historical Society.*

Photo Frederick Eberstadt.

On reaching the drive the promenader crosses to the statue of Daniel Webster, 1876, by Thomas Ball. Originally the site was an island in the middle of the drive, but the part of the drive on the Lake side was converted from asphalt to turf, a sort of "man bites dog" twist in park planning.

To the northwest of the Webster statue there is still an island of greenery surrounded by drives. It was here that Olmsted and Vaux, planned to have the park's "Refectory" or restaurant. Within easy reach of the 72nd Street entrance and accessible via the drives, the site also had the advantage of a commanding position overlooking the Lake and the Ramble and was sheltered from the prevailing winds.

The promenader goes right, on the path at the edge of the Lake. Through the trees he will catch a glimpse, across the water, of a small rustic landing beneath a large turkey oak (*Quercus cerris*). The Lake originally had six such landings, each of a different design. Four have been reinstated. The path turns up to Cherry Hill Concourse, where carriage drivers would pause to let their horses refresh themselves at the fountain in the center. The fountain has been dry for years, although there are plans to restore it. The Concourse is presently a parking lot.

To the left of the path around the Concourse is a clump of eastern hemlock (*Tsuga canadensis*), the first evergreens encountered on this tour. Formerly such clumps were found in many places in the park. Soot and car fumes have contributed to a great decrease in their number. Deciduous trees, producing a fresh crop of leaves every spring, suffer much less from the city's noxious air. Beyond the hemlocks are some fine cut-leaf European beeches (*Fagus sylvatica* var. *incisa*).

At the Lake the promenader's eye will be taken by the western skyline. In summer the trees conceal the gables of the old Dakota, but, to the north can be seen at all times the twin towers of the San Remo with their circular temples. Next, continuing right, comes the low red granite tower with the green copper ball of the American Museum of Natural History, then the substantial Beresford, and, far to the north, the high Eldorado Towers.

From a wintry day in 1858 when a little water was let into the not yet completed Lake so that skating could begin, this basin of water has been the most used and appreciated park feature. After the Lake's completion skating became the rage

Skating on the Lake in 1865 by J. Culverhouse. The Terrace is to the left, the Bow Bridge in the background. The summerhouse on the hill has disappeared. *J. Clarence Davies Collection, Museum of the City of New York.*

in New York; such crowds swarmed upon the ice in the park that empty lots all over town were flooded and private rinks established to accommodate the enthusiasts. An annual report of the park describes the Lake scene:

> *It is certain that about 80,000 persons visited the Park on one day, and half of this number were probably together at one time on and about the twenty acres of ice, the larger part moving rapidly, in exuberant spirits, while the roads were crowded with carriages. . . . It is undeniable, that the concentration of such numbers of pleasure-seekers upon the little space of twenty acres, while it imposes some restraint*

upon the skaters, and calls for constant exercise of skill to avoid collisions, adds vastly to the general gayety, and thus causes an excitement of healthful hilarity which, if it can be enjoyed in safety, is in itself of no small value. None of the various exhibitions of crowded life of this metropolis are more interesting, or can be viewed with more unmingled satisfaction than the skating scene upon the park.

When the Lake ice was ready to welcome skaters, horsecars coming to the park broke out flags, and from a belltower on Vista Rock, now the site of the Belvedere Castle, was hoisted a red ball. Calcium reflectors provided light for night skating, temporary skating houses were placed at the Lake's edge, and a corner of the northern part of the Lake was reserved exclusively for ladies. For those persons too fragile or clumsy to skate, ice chairs with runners could be hired. Park attendance reached its peak, not on the hottest summer squelcher but on a frosty winter day when the ice sparkled and snow piled up on the drives through which sleighs could crunch. The Scottish sport of curling was also practiced on the Lake.

Warmer winters and artificial rinks have robbed the Lake of its colorful skating throng, but in the clement season, it still offers the cheerful spectacle of the Central Park navy afloat. The first boats were put on the Lake in 1860; a year later one Thomas S. Dick was put in charge of the concession, agreeing to maintain from May to November of each year two classes of boats—a "passage" or omnibus boat that left the Terrace stairs every fifteen minutes on a circuit of the Lake, stopping at the six landings to pick up and discharge passengers for a fare of 10 cents, and private or call boats hired by the hour. Because of his knowledge of the patrons of the private boats, Mr. Dick became considered an expert on the progress of New York romances. The "passage" boats were first oar-propelled, then replaced by steam launches and finally by electric launches in existence up to forty years ago. A gondola was also part of the Lake scene well into this century.

Photo J.S. Johnston. New-York Historical Society.

Walking to the Terrace in 1894 and in 1966. The siting of the present boathouse is far more conspicuous than the old one. Note how the buildings on Fifth Avenue have shot above the tree line.

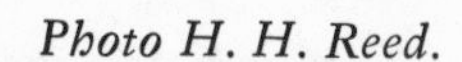

Photo H. H. Reed.

The first one, given to the park in 1862, lay idle for some time, a gondolier not accompanying the gift. In the 1890's boating was customary at night. "Here and there the single red light of a boat shines out as it passes," runs one description, "sending its gleam across the water, or a gondola, gay with red and green lights, moves by to the tinkling of a mandolin and the song of the gondolier." As late as 1934 a "Venetian Water Carnival" was held here.

The Lake's original 22½ acres of water have shrunk in recent years thanks to "improvements" near the West 77th Street entrance. An elbow of the Lake, extending from the line of 75th to 78th streets, between the drive and the bridle path was partially filled in as a concession to those who wanted to do away with all water in the park when a malaria scare gripped the city in the 1880's. The branch remained, however, until 1940, when it was completely filled, following departmental policy.

Across the Lake to the north the promenader will see a very small island, at one time considerably larger; it is the only surviving island of the three that existed in the park's lakes and ponds. To the left, on the Hernshead, a spit of land on the Lake's western edge, sits the Ladies Pavilion, or "Ombra." It is not, as might be supposed, one of the original Lake landings but an attractive cast-iron shelter moved to this spot from Columbus Circle.

Continuing on the path along the Lake, the promenader goes by some Austrian pines (*Pinus nigra*) on the right and, on the left, near the bridge a southern catalpa (*Catalpa bignonioides*). Bow Bridge, 1859, by Calvert Vaux, leading to the Ramble (see below) is of cast iron and is much admired by fanciers of the metal. To the right, opposite the bridge approach, is a large bur oak (*Quercus macrocarpa*), surrounded by erosion. To the south of it are several tulip trees (*Liriodendron tulipifera*), which gain their name from tulip-shaped blossoms. The bur oak, by the way, was here at the turn of the century. This cannot be said of most of Central Park's planting, when it is compared to the planting of the early 1900's as listed in an informative book, *Trees and Shrubs of Central Park* by Louis Harmon Peet. There used to be a great range of species in the park. Prospect Park, by comparison, still offers a variety of sixty-year-old planting, and in almost every way has fared better than her older Manhattan sister. But then, Prospect Park has many fewer visitors, and equally important, it does not suffer the quantity of traffic. The annual 12,000,000 visitors to Central Park, a figure five times the maximum considered satisfactory by the National Recreation Association, present almost insurmountable problems in maintaining planting, turf and facilities.

The path along the Lake runs between weeping willows (*Salix babylonica*) and a variety of Japanese flowering cherry (*Prunus serrulata*). At the Terrace the promenader has a pleasant spot to pause. (The tour continues from the Terrace after the description of the East Side entrance.)

EAST SIDE ENTRANCE

Transportation: For Fifth Avenue and 72nd Street: 68th Street Station of East Side IRT Subway. Madison and Fifth Avenue Bus Lines.

The alternate or East Side entrance to this tour is at the Inventors Gate, 72nd Street and Fifth Avenue. The planting on Fifth Avenue, a double row of American elms, is hard to keep in good condition because of the ravages of the Dutch elm disease. In some spots, the elm is being replaced by the honey locust. On entering the park by the north path the promenader will observe the shiny-leafed *Euonymus kiautschovica.* Here it is backed by Cornelian cherry (*Cornus mas*), a small tree that is covered in early spring with yellow flowers. Across the drive to the south, surrounded by a fence, is one of the oldest trees in the park, presumably the oldest Chinese elm (*Ulmus parvifolia*) in the country. This fine tree, recognizable by its small leaves, opens late in spring, with the result that the Park Department gets letters and calls to do something about "that dying tree."

The promenader should take the first turn north; the shrub-like trees to the left are spindle trees (*Euonymus alatus*) with corky wings on the branches. They are accompanied by Downy Hawthorn (*Crataegus mollis*) and Washington Hawthorn (*C. phaenopyrum*). The path descends, via the left fork, to Conservatory Water (or pond). Along the way are Norway maples (*Acer platanoides*) of the variety called *schwedleri;* they are particularly conspicuous in springtime when their large leaves are a reddish purple. If the East Side skyline, rising over the "green wall" is not as picturesque as the West Side with its towers, the unconscious *sharawadgi* is enlivened by penthouse terraces bursting with shrubbery and an occasional tree. The pond gets its name from the conservatory originally planned to overlook its eastern shore. Although foundations were laid in the 1860's, the building was never put up. A Conservatory was eventually opened in the Northern Section of the park in 1899.

Arriving at the pond's edge the promenader has before him one of the more reassuring vistas of the park. On a good day the blue water is alive with small sails, and the shoreline crowded with youngsters. The Kerbs Memorial Model Boathouse, a gift to the park, was built in 1954 on the designs of Aymar Embury II. Visitors without model sailboats can rent them at the Boathouse.

Overlooking the pond are two statues, rather misguided philanthropic bequests, placed here in the 1950's. To the north is the Alice-in-Wonderland group by José de Creeft, a memorial presented by George Delacorte, and to the west the

Conservatory Water in the 1890's by William Merritt Chase.
New York Public Library.

Hans Christian Andersen Memorial Statue by George Lober, given by the Danish people. Where the latter statue stands, there was once a cascade. Much is made of the fact that children love these statues, but children love the park anyway. A lily pond was placed in a depression to the northeast of the pond in the 1880's. Floating in it were Egyptian lotuses, purple and red Zanzibar lilies, deep red Indian lilies, rose-colored Cape Cod lilies and other water plants.

The tour goes west, taking the path at the southwest corner of Conservatory Water between pin oaks, London planes and Norway maples. It then goes under Trefoil Arch, designed by Vaux, reaching the other side without having to cross the drive at this point. To the right is the 72nd Street Central Park Boathouse, given to the park by the Loebs, a well-known banking family. Built in 1954, it is the third boathouse on the Lake. The previous two of wood were in the rustic manner, a style traditional in the park until recently. A snack bar here and a sheltered terrace overlooking the Lake make it a favorite resort for many. Unfortunately the cheerful spot is marred by the blacktop of a parking lot and an overabundance of link-chain or hurricane-wire fencing. The visitor should continue southwest on the path along the border of the Lake to the Terrace.

At this point the East and West side tours meet, to continue as one.

The Terrace is one of the more popular gathering places in the park. Those who are familiar with it from fashion photographs—models regularly take a variety of awkward stances before the camera here—might be astonished to see the crowds of a summer Sunday afternoon. With the fountain splashing, the Lake filled with boats, the scene is wonderful,

> *all classes largely represented with a common purpose* [to quote Olmsted], *not at all intellectual, competitive with none, disposing to jealousy and spiritual or intellectual pride toward none, each individual adding by his mere presence to the pleasure of all others; all helping to the greater happiness of each. You may thus often see vast numbers of persons brought closely together, poor and rich, young and old, Jew and Gentile. . . . Is it doubtful that it does men good to come together in this way in pure air and under the light of heaven?*

The general design of the Terrace, completed in 1864, was done by Calvert Vaux, the detail by Jacob Wrey Mould, another architect, who did much work in the park. The style is part Gothic, part Romanesque, while the ornament is natural or realistic. (Mould had spent ten years in Spain with Owen Jones, author of the influential *Grammar of Ornament* and a

The Trefoil Arch at the East Drive in the late 1860's. The steps lead up to the Lake. Children are seen playing on a gravel path.

New-York Historical Society.

book on the Alhambra.) The central element of the Terrace is the Bethesda Fountain, topped by "The Angel of the Waters" of the Gospel of Saint John, Chapter 5:

> *Now there is at Jerusalem by the sheep market a pool, which is called in the Hebrew tongue Bethesda, having five porches. In these lay a great multitude of impotent folk, of blind, halt,*

withered, waiting for the moving of the water. For an angel went down at a certain season into the pool, and troubled the water: whosoever then first after troubling the water stepped in was made whole of whatsoever disease he had.

The statues are the work of Emma Stebbins, one of several American sculptresses with studios in Rome in the last century. She may have been the model for Hilda, a character in Nathaniel Hawthorne's novel, *The Marble Faun.* Miss Stebbins sent some sketches to Mould and was given the commission; her brother was Park Commissioner Henry G. Stebbins. Completed in 1865, cast in Munich in 1871, the statues of the Bethesda Fountain were unveiled in 1873. Beneath "The Angel of the Waters" stand "Temperance," "Purity," "Health" and "Peace," fit subjects for nineteenth-century Americans who would hardly tolerate a large triton or an Aphrodite in a public park.

Across the Lake from the Terrace is the previously mentioned Ramble, the most intricately planted section of the park, well worth a separate visit.

In the Greenward text, Olmsted and Vaux explained why they chose the site and what they planned to do with it:

It is well sheltered, and large masses of rock occur at intervals. The soil is moist, and altogether remarkably well adapted to what is called in Europe an American garden—that is, a ground for the special cultivation of hardy plants of the natural order Ericacaei, *consisting of rhododendrons, andromedas, azaleas, kalmias, rhodoras, etc. The present growth, consisting of sweet-gum, spice-bush, tulip-tree, sassafras, red-maple, black-oak, azalea, andromeda, etc. is exceedingly intricate and interesting. The ground is at present too much encumbered with stone, and with various indifferent plants. By clearing these away, and carefully leaving what is valuable; by making suitable paths, planting abundantly, as above suggested, and introducing fastigiate shrubs and evergreens occasionally, to prevent a monotony of bushes, the place may be made charming. . . .*

The Bank Rock Bridge, formerly the Oak Bridge, leads to the Ramble from the west. Iron pipe railing has replaced oak, and boats can no longer enter Bank Rock Bay.

Museum of the City of New York.

Visitors in the 1860's coming to study the Ramble's charms usually entered the area by crossing the Oak Bridge, which spanned the western bay of the Lake, Bank Rock Bay in line with 77th Street. Iron has replaced the fanciful oak railing of the bridge, but a path still leads through the narrow, picturesque Stone Arch. Until 1929 a branch of the path descended stone steps to the interior of a cave, opening onto a shallow inlet of the Lake. The Cave, a picturesque invention devised by Olmsted and Vaux, is now walled off.

A meandering brook, the Gill, survives in the Ramble, as does a rustic summerhouse on the crown of a hill; but long gone are the occasional stork, crane, heron and pelican that were placed along the waterway, as well as the peacocks and guinea fowl who once strutted the small lawns. Native bird life, however, still flourishes in this area. During the spring migration period, bird watchers, including organized groups

Museum of the City of New York.

The Cave from the Lake a century ago. Promenaders could enter the Cave from the land side to the north. The Cave no longer exists and, as can be seen from today's photograph, the branch of the Lake that led to the south entrance is silted.

led by a staff member of the American Museum of Natural History, clamber up and down the slopes. As many as thirty species of warbler have been spotted in the Ramble on a single day in May. (See Appendix D for dates of migration.) Among the birds that have come to nest in the park are sparrow hawk, flicker, robin, wood thrush, grackle, blue jay, catbird, cardinal, song sparrow and downy woodpecker.

Photo Frederick Eberstadt.

The Ramble is as interesting to the botanist as it is to the bird watcher. The planting is profuse, many different trees and shrubs being represented, including nannyberry, Hupeh evodia, Amur cork tree, Chinese pagoda tree, Kentucky coffee tree, persimmon, green ash, Siberian elm, cucumber magnolia, meadowsweet, and shagbark hickory.

How an old people's center nearly got placed in the hilly Ramble is one of the more absurd stories of recent park history. In 1955, a foundation offered $250,000 for this project, which was to include a recreation building complete with television, horseshoe and croquet lots, shuffleboard, a service building, parking lot and yards of hurricane-wire fencing—all to be reached by a seven-story climb from a special bus stop at the 79th Street Transverse Road. The Park Department agreed to accept the gift, and the project might have come into being had not a violent public protest gone up. The Ramble's main defender was the Linnaean Society, whose

Surveying the scene from the rustic Shadow Bridge in the Ramble in the early days of the Park. The same setting today.

New-York Historical Society.

chief concern is wild fowl. Luckily, the foundation, sensitive to adverse publicity, withdrew its donation. Soon after, the Ramble was rehabilitated at a cost of $200,000, which also paid for an enlarged parking lot. New planting, new benches, a scoured brook, topsoil and manure were part of the project, and yet, due to the lack of maintenance little evidence of the work exists today.

Enjoying the view of the Ramble from the Terrace, the promenader can savor the joy Olmsted and Vaux had in transforming the once barren acres. "*J'ai encore acheté plusieurs*

Photo Frederick Eberstadt.

terres, à qui j'ai dit à la manière accoutumée: 'Je vous fais parc'. . . ." ("I have again bought several pieces of land, to whom I said in the accustomed manner: 'I make you park. . . .' "), wrote Madame de Sévigné about transforming her country place, and so the two designers could have said about this rocky part of Manhattan. Perhaps the Prince de Ligne, eighteenth-century statesman and amateur gardener, best defined the rewards of landscaping: "A stay in the country is made never more pleasant than by beholding woods, fields and water daily assume new shape on command."

At one time, two high poles rose from the decorated posts that stand at the lake end of the Terrace, or "Esplanade" as this area is sometimes called. From the poles floated brightly colored gonfalons, long banners with tassels, one bearing the arms of the city, the other the arms of the state.

The Terrace has always been a popular spot; the date in this instance is 1872. In the background stands one of a pair of posts with gonfalons. Engraving after a picture by C. Rosenberg.

New York Public Library.

The big change at the Terrace has been in the planting. In the 1890's there was formal bedding on the slopes at the sides, and the emphasis was on evergreens (as was true of the planting of so much of the park). Portugal laurel, common cherry laurel, cotoneaster, Acuba, Leucothoe, mountain laurel, arborvitae, and several varieties of rhododendron and azalea were the evergreens. There were also Scotch laburnum, English hawthorn, spiraea, Austrian brier rose and even yuccas. By the 1900's the bedding had gone and much of the evergreen. The Persian lilac, the Guelder rose, the saucer magnolia, honeysuckle, the General Jacqueminot rose and rose of Sharon were the plants plus English yew and European holly, representing the few evergreens. Only rhododendron and azalea offer a link to the past. Today the planting is chiefly pin oak, with azaleas near the drive. At the turn of the century the basin of the Bethesda Fountain held plantations of lotus and lily set out in underwater tubs.

The promenader, strolling toward the Terrace arcade to the south, comes upon an obscure bronze plaque, embedded in the floor of the Esplanade. It tells the beholder that he is standing on the Navy Terrace, so named in 1947 to honor the Navy dead of the two World Wars. Name changing has become increasingly popular as an "economy memorial"; it has the advantage of costing the sponsors neither effort nor money but hardly does honor to the purpose. The name-change, in this instance, has never caught on. In recognition of the artistic merits of the Terrace and the Bethesda Fountain a landmark plaque was placed by the New York Community Trust in 1965 on the left wall leading to the arcade.

To either side of the arcade, flights of steps lead directly to the drive; the ornament of the stair posts still displays the intricacy of Mould's naturalistic detail, more of which can be seen on the large reliefs on the upper part of the stair railing. On the reliefs facing into the arcade, birds in full relief fly about and perch on branches of horse chestnuts, sycamores and other plants. The yellow trim of the Terrace consists of Albert freestone from New Brunswick, Canada.

By using the Terrace Bridge Arcade, the promenader avoids crossing the drive and has, besides, the opportunity to see the Minton tile roof lining made in England from designs of Mould. In the course of the park's history, snacks have sometimes been served in the arcade, and from 1934 to 1956 tables, shaded by umbrellas, were set out on the Esplanade. A large Fountain Café, closed during the winter, was inaugurated on the same spot in 1966. Olmsted objected to using the arcade for dispensing refreshments, complaining that it had not been designed to this end; what he had in mind was a cool open shelter as a refuge from the summer's heat. Olmsted and Vaux also thought in terms of a formal setting to underscore one of the finest views in the park.

Beyond the arcade, steps take the promenader to the Mall, which stretches 1,212 feet to the south. On either side of the steps are posts of Albert freestone with small reliefs. On the right they represent the scholar, one having an open book and lamp, another an owl, and a third evoking night by a (now headless) witch on a broom and by a jack-o'-lantern. The post on the left has three reliefs representing the farmer, one showing a barnyard scene with a sickle and a sheaf of wheat, the second a rooster, and the third a rising sun. If the visitor turns back and looks north, he can make out the Belvedere Castle tower; the park's planners designed the Mall's axis to point at Vista Rock, the hill on which the Castle stands. Meteorological apparatus rises from the Belvedere's tower. Since 1919, the Castle has housed one of the city's weather bureaus, previously in the Arsenal. "Current temperature reading in Central Park . . ." is a familiar refrain to most of New York's radio and TV listeners.

The drive at this point was one of the best spots to watch the great parade of carriages roll by—the park's most fashionable sight from its opening until automobiles were permitted use of the drives. In the fall of 1860 when carriages entering

The great parade of carriages on the drive near the Terrace in 1883.
Harper's Weekly. *New-York Historical Society.*

the drive at 59th Street were partially obscured under a cloud of dust gathered on the unpaved Fifth and Eighth avenues, the *Herald* recorded,

> *It is not uncommon to find from three to four thousand people driving over the Central Park in costly equipages of all shapes in one day at this delightful season, and as many as four hundred finely mounted equestrians of both sexes* [*the bridle path was not finished until 1862, but equestrians always had use of the drive*]. *Every quality of animal, from the showy and steady roadster to the fastest blood horse, can be seen there, and every build of vehicle from the sulky to the dashing four-in-hand carriage. It would not be too much to say that the cash value of one day's turn-out in the Park and on Bloomingdale Road* [*Broadway*], *both in animals and equipages, is not far from a quarter of a million dollars. Every class of society, too—moneyed society, we mean—is represented there. . . .*

Visitors from abroad taken to see the park, the city's biggest tourist attraction of the time, were impressed both by the park and the procession on the drives. A young Frenchman jotted in his journal in 1864:

My friends took me to Central Park, a vast American "Bois de Boulogne," with its valleys, rocks, cascades, bridges, aqueducts, lakes and cliffs, spreading out from the end of Fifth Avenue. . . . Nothing is more American than this ambitious name, given at first sight to wild terrain outside the City. . . . All is new, hardly finished, yet already it swarms each evening with horsemen and carriages, especially those remarkable American vehicles whose slender wheels resemble filigreed jewelry. . . .

Later on the park even merited praise from the usually supercilious English. A lady novelist from London after an American visit in 1881 bubbled:

Central Park is the only place where you can enjoy a drive—there driving is a delight, the roads are simply perfect, and scores of splendid equipages and beautiful women are on view daily in the grand drives from three till six o'clock; while the bridle paths, winding through sylvan shades beneath full-foliaged trees, are crowded with fair equestrians and their attendant cavaliers. . . . New York is very proud of Central Park; and well it may be so, for it is one of the finest in the world, there is nothing like it this side of the Atlantic. Twenty years ago it was a mere swampy waste, now it is a triumph of engineering skill and a splendid illustration of the genius of landscape gardening: there are smooth green lawns, shady groves, lakes, beautifully wooded dells and vine-covered arbours; whichever way you turn you come upon delicious bits of picturesque scenery blossoming in unexpected nooks and corners. Here and there huge grey rocks stand in their original rugged majesty, their broken lichen-covered boulders tumbling at their base.

Thanks to the park, style and action in horseflesh replaced speed, and a variety of carriages from spider wagons to breaks, never before seen on Fifth Avenue, replaced the sulky for driving. August Belmont was conceded to have the best turnout; "handling the ribbons himself" he drove his English break with four horses, a pair of bays and a pair of blacks; William Cullen Bryant favored a fast gray with a light wagon. Among the many driving into the park at 59th Street were the publishers Harper and Appleton, Peter Cooper and numerous Astors. (Commodore Vanderbilt stayed with the fast drivers who congregated on Bloomingdale Road around 90th Street.) The equestrians included the banker's wife, Mrs. August Belmont, Mrs. James Gordon Bennett, wife of the owner of the *Herald*, Henry J. Raymond of *The New York Times*, on a white horse, and the historian George Bancroft. Carriage driving in the park was not fashionable until midafternoon. The equestrians would use the bridle path in the morning, returning in the afternoon to join the carriages on the drive.

After 1869, public omnibuses plied the drives, charging 25 cents for a tour of the park. Carriage occupants, equestrians and pedestrians enjoyed the sight of each other so much that they clamored in the 1870's for greater proximity—for duplication of Hyde Park's "Rotten Row," a short, straight promenade with the drive, bridle path and walk side by side. When consulted on the possibility of creating a "Rotten Row," Olmsted answered that the narrow park provided no feasible economical site. The straightest part of the drive, which borders the eastern edge of the Reservoir, was used as a "Rotten Row" of sorts but did not serve the purpose well, there being no pedestrian path to the east of the drive at that time. (Mrs. Russell Sage greatly added to the attractiveness of this stretch of the drive in the 1910's by donating $70,000 for the planting of rhododendrons.)

Unfortunately no New York artist caught the grand parade on the drives, nor evoked gold-plate New York as Constantin

Guy's wash drawings of carriages and horses evoked Second Empire Paris with the vividness of Offenbach's music. American painters of horseflesh, namely Frederic Remington and Charles E. Russell, were out West although at one point the former sketched Central Park equestrians for *Harper's Weekly*. William Merritt Chase was fond of painting both Central and Prospect parks, and Maurice Prendergast, Edward Hopper and Gifford Beal sketched Central Park occasionally. The park, it must be confessed, has been poorly served by the artist; only Leon Kroll has captured the pastoral element of the park landscape and executed it in classical terms.

"Sleep" by Leon Kroll, the Park's best artist.

Fitchburg Art Museum, on loan from the National Academy of Design.

The promenader should turn south and look down the Mall. Two fountains, gilded birdcages, and a pair of fanciful drinking fountains once stood in this area in front of the steps. The classical Band Shell to the east was designed in 1923 by William G. Tachau and given to the park by Elkan Naumburg, who had financed a series of park concerts for years. The first park concert was performed in 1859. A graceful iron bandstand, richly decorated, was designed by Jacob Wrey Mould. The colors included sky-blue, lime-ogee, pea-green, indigo-blue and red; the roof, standing on six red posts, was lined inside with arabesques and escutcheons inscribed with the names of composers; the cupola was of Clark blue with a sprinkling of gilt stars. Completed in 1862, it was placed to

A sunny afternoon near one of the fountains, formerly at the north end of the Mall. Painted in 1913 by Gifford Beal.

Photo Peter A. Juley & Son.

The old Bandstand by Jacob Wrey Mould. It stood to the west of the present Band Shell. *Avery Library, Columbia University.*

the west of the Mall. "This site [for the bandstand] is recommended," Olmsted and Vaux wrote, "because it is conspicuous without being obtrusive, and is easy of access from the promenade [the Mall] and from one of the leading avenue entrances; while to the north it commands from its terraces and verandas the finest views that are to be obtained in the lower part of the park." A floating bandstand for the Lake was also designed by Mould. It was never built, but a ten-man cornet band would occasionally give concerts from a boat, promenaders both on the Terrace and in the Ramble being within earshot of the music.

Currently the Guggenheim Memorial Concerts are presented several evenings a week from mid-June to mid-August by the Goldman Band, alternating with other musical entertainment. And there is no greater delight than to sit or wander here, listening to the music. The park gained another great musical attraction in 1965; the New York Philharmonic now plays four concerts a summer from a portable band shell, set up on the edge of the Sheep Meadow. During the first season 20,000 people jammed the meadow for each performance.

Incidentally, the park's other free summer evening attraction, the fine plays presented by the New York Shakespeare Festival, are performed in a structure that is certainly not in the Olmsted and Vaux tradition. The Delacorte Theatre, built in 1962 on the western shore of Belvedere Lake (the last vestige of the Old Reservoir) could not be more conspicuous, painted as it is in bright green, an enormous steel light tower looming at its rear. The elephantine structure and equipment cost the city $225,000; the donor provided $150,000. It is now used only during the summer season. There have been proposals to enclose it, making possible year-

Music on the Lake. The cornet band plays away aboard a canopied boat in 1865. *Harper's Weekly.* *New-York Historical Society.*

round use—a threat that would only compound the original error. Part of the delight of summer theatre in a park is the natural setting, an advantage sacrificed here.

The tour goes east and up a flight of steps next to the Band Shell, reaching the Pergola, a rustic arbor covered by Chinese wisteria. In the old days the public would sit here listening to the music played from the old Bandstand and so would the occupants of carriages assembled on the Concourse then to the east of the Pergola. This opportunity was lost with construction of the Band Shell; also lost was the pleasure of viewing the crowded Mall below. Now, a break in the viburnum hedge bordering the Pergola opens onto the Mary Harriman Rumsey Playground, presented in 1936 by the sister of Governor W. Averell Harriman. The Playground is built on the site of the Concourse and of the Casino, a restaurant remembered as one of the gayest spots of the 1920's.

With its cover charge, expensive menu and sumptuous interior decoration by Joseph Urban, the Casino was frequented by a fast set, including the high-living Mayor James J. Walker. Parties would take place there before a midnight sailing, and, if the mayor was a guest he might offer a police escort to speed the travelers to the departing steamer. With the advent of the reforming Fusion administration in 1934, the Casino was doomed; ex-Mayor Walker had left a large unpaid tab.

Ironically, the Vaux-designed Casino, put up in 1864, had been intended as a refreshment center for women and children. The park designers protested its use by the general public. While it is possible to condone its destruction, since buildings are on sufferance in the park, its replacement by a playground was senseless. This spot is reached only by crossing the East Drive, and because there is no shade to be had, the playground receives few visitors. The donor and the park would have been better served by the planting of a clump of trees.

The promenader continues through the Pergola to the south and returns to the Mall. The oak grove to the left, at the turn of the path, is a World War I Memorial to the 307th Infantry Regiment as an inscribed boulder nearby reveals. The small cement blocks with bronze plaques are part of the same memorial. Beyond, a headstone recalls the World War I dead of the Knights of Pythias. It can easily be seen why such objects were kept out of the park in the early days, for the grounds would soon have been littered with them. Since the policy against placing memorials in the parks continues, it may well be asked where their place should be in the city. Cemeteries, thought to be the proper location for monuments in the 1860's, are no longer the object of the New Yorker's Sunday afternoon promenade. With its relentless gridiron, the city has too few squares, circles and irregular street corners for statues, and those available have largely been preempted. Ideally, there should be one or possibly several "Battle Abbeys" where such memorials could be properly sheltered and where ample space could be left available for future memorials, in the form of a wall plaque, relief, or sculptural group. Such a "Pantheon" might become a place of pilgrimage where the fallen could be dutifully honored.

Not long after the park opened, the city of Philadelphia presented it with eight deer, and a deer paddock was established on the present Memorial Grove site. Grazing animals were considered a natural complement to the picturesque landscape. (Dublin's Phoenix Park still has a herd of deer.) Farther north in the park there was a pasturage for horned cattle—a motley crew composed of moose, African buffalo, and English, Irish and Spanish beef cattle. The Park Commissioners got so carried away by bovinity that they planned at one time to build what they termed a "vacherie," to display all available breeds of milch cattle for the education of visiting farmers. This project was quickly abandoned, but the commissioners, deluged by gifts of animals, including white mice,

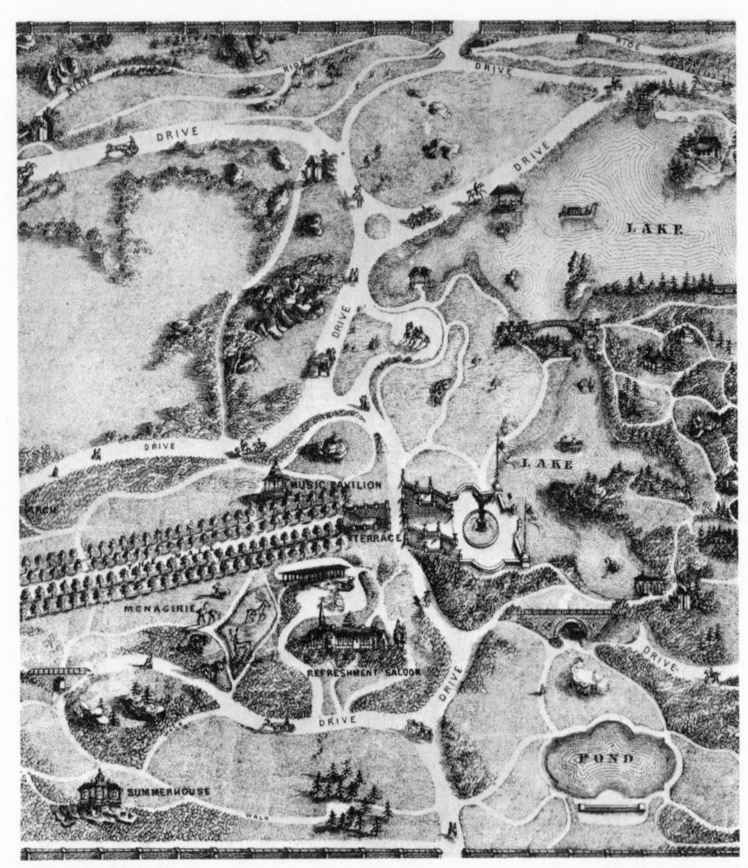

A section of an 1865 map with elevations of shelters, pavilions and other structures completed to that year. *New York Public Library.*

were forced to provide an animal refuge. As a temporary solution they chose the ground floor of the Arsenal and the immediate surroundings. Olmsted and Vaux always fought having a menagerie within the park, suggesting first it be placed in Manhattan Square. This site, however, was soon preempted by the Museum of Natural History, which moved there from temporary quarters in the upper floors of the Arsenal. The North Meadow was then proposed as a suitable place for the animals, but after bitter controversy the idea was dismissed. While the menagerie was to remain at the Arsenal, though not in it, it did not become truly permanent until 1934 when the present brick complex was built and the "Menagerie" became the "Zoo."

Another educational enterprise entered into by the Park Commissioners resulted in dinosaur models being buried, like hidden treasure, somewhere in the park. An English sculptor, B. Waterhouse Hawkins, was commissioned to come to this country to construct huge models of the ancient beasts, and foundations for a Paleozoic Museum were laid near the park's western edge, at 63rd Street. The "Tweed Ring," gaining control of park management in 1870, decided the project was worthless, filled in the foundations and presumably buried the models Mr. Hawkins had completed.

The tour continues south down the Mall, which is bordered by American elms, most of the present ones planted in 1919.

> *Although averse on general principles to a symmetrical arrangement of trees* [*wrote the park's designers*], *we consider it an essential feature of a metropolitan park that it should contain a grand promenade, level, spacious and thoroughly shaded. . . . The objection to which it is liable is that it divides the landscape into two parts, and it is therefore desirable to decide at what point this necessity can be submitted to with the least sacrifice to the general effect. The whole topographical character of the park is so varied, so suggestive of natural treatment, so picturesque, so individual in its characteristics, that it would be contrary to common sense to make the avenue its leading feature, or to occupy any great extent of ground for this special purpose. It must be subservient to the general design, if that general design is to be in accordance with the present configuration of the ground, and we have therefore thought that it should, so far as possible, be complete in itself, and not became a portion of*

any of the leading drives . . . and we can find no better place for such a grand mall, or open air hall of reception, as we desire to have, than the ground before us.

What lay before the designers was a swampy area that had to be filled in with rocks blasted from other parts of the park. The view north up the Mall to the Belvedere framed by the arch of elms is not as impressive as it once was. The elms planted on turf originally continued in a solid line almost to the steps leading down to the Terrace Arcade. Today the perspective is ruined by the ungainly galvanized-iron lampposts and the wide expanse of asphalt on the Mall in front of the Band Shell.

Among the diversions once offered on the Mall were children's carriages drawn by pairs of goats commanded by a liveried attendant. A camel, the first animal in the park to provide children's rides, had a much rougher existence than

The camel mowing a park lawn. *Harper's Weekly.*
New York Public Library.

the goats; he was sometimes hitched to a mower and used to cut the grass. Donkeys replaced the dromedary as the children's beast of burden, and today ponies dutifully pull carts around a new track, southeast of the Zoo. The modern pony carts present rather a curious spectacle with their rubber tires, their tall un-uniformed attendants riding rather than pacing alongside.

On and around the Mall are numerous statues, for this was the only place originally intended for such works. (An appendix lists information on all statues and monuments found in the park.) One of the better known is that of Balto, the leader of the husky team that mushed its way to Nome bringing diphtheria serum in 1925. The noble dog is to the east of the Mall on the other side of Willowdell Arch. The work of

Builders of the park on the Willowdell Bridge east of the Mall. On the far left stands Frederick Law Olmsted, next to him Calvert Vaux.

Photo Victor Prevost. Stuart Collection, New York Public Library.

Frederick G. R. Roth, it was completed in 1925. Balto's bronze back glistens from the polish given it by child riders.

Continuing to the end of the Mall, the promenader will come upon the location originally chosen for the equestrian statue of General Sherman, now placed at the Grand Army Plaza, Fifth Avenue and 59th Street. As planned with elaborate balustrades and steps, the monument would have taken up almost two acres. Samuel Parsons objected violently to the plan, pointing out that the statue would block one of the best and most carefully designed views in the park. He won his case as he had about a decade before when it was proposed to place Grant's Tomb off the Mall.

One statue worth visiting is J. Q. A. Ward's "Indian Hunter," reached by the path to the west. Decorative rather than commemorative, this is the finest piece of sculpture in the park, and it has been the most popular since its unveiling in 1869. The Indian is a perfect example of skillful modeling, of vigor of stance and of delineation of muscle. (Today's sculptural nudes are either muscleless or muscle-bound.) And the dog is wonderfully alive. Largely because Ward is preeminently a classical sculptor, he has been forgotten today.

Northwest of the statue is a wide strip of asphalt, formerly part of the drive. Park officials should be commended for their action in closing this stretch to traffic in 1936. Traffic has also been barred from three other stretches of the drive: one from Columbus Circle to the West Drive, a second at 79th Street to the East Drive, and the third to the north of the North Meadow. Bicyclists and roller skaters use the obsolete drive west of the Mall, but the park, which has suffered so much asphalt in this century, would benefit if it could be turned back to lawn. The closing of four unnecessary stretches of the drive was certainly a step in the right direction. The next step might be removal of lesser used access roads, and their replacement by turf as was done with two spurs of the drive in the 1930's.

Between the Mall and the abandoned drive, stand, somewhere, two royal trees. In 1860 the Prince of Wales planted here an English oak and an American elm; the latter reportedly survives. Edward Albert, Prince of Wales, grandson of Albert Edward, carried on the family tradition by planting an elm in the same region in 1919.

The promenader goes south to cross the drive by the statue of Columbus. Olmsted and Vaux, it might be assumed, neglected to provide a tunnel under the drive at this busy crossing. Actually, the Marble Arch was found here until the 1930's. With its fountain and benches, this arch, considered the most elegant one in the park, offered a place of rest and refreshment on a hot day. But it was allowed to decay and was eliminated altogether after 1934. The path goes southeast alongside the drive, to take the bridge over the 65th Street Transverse Road. With the spreading blacktop, no attempt has been made to keep up the planting, and the road below, formerly concealed, is now too plainly in view. A worthwhile "improvement," which could have been undertaken in the past decades, is the covering over of all the transverse roads in the park. Had all the money, public and philanthropic, spent on playgrounds, fencing, new structures, roads and other "improvements," been spent on bridging the transverse roads, the park would have gained enormously in natural space.

The promenader takes the path to the right to pass the Dairy, designed by Calvert Vaux in Gothic Revival and completed in 1870. The building, shorn about 1955 of a handsome wooden canopy over the path, was intended to serve fresh milk and other light refreshments to children, for whom the surrounding area was planned. It is now used as a storage shed. Cows, to furnish milk, and a few other barnyard animals were tethered in the vicinity and stabled in a building to the southeast, known as the Children's Cottage which disappeared long ago. The "Tweed Ring" complained in 1870 that the Dairy was not generally accessible, did their best to expose it to view, and made use of it as an all-purpose refreshment stand.

The path drops down to the left and passes on the right the

hill site of the Kinderberg, another component of the old children's area, which was once topped by a large vine-covered rustic shelter, now by an unimaginative brick Chess and Checkers House, financed by a gift from the late Bernard Baruch in 1952. The present Kinderberg is mostly used by elderly men.

The walk continues down the slope until it joins another, running east-west; this path was once the eastern spur of the present bridle path, which now ends at a point north of Seventh Avenue. (Winding around the Zoo, the former bridle path came out at 59th Street and Fifth Avenue.) To the south of the path stands the Wollman Memorial Skating Rink, taking the place of the northern arm of the Pond, the principal ornament of the park's southern end.

> *To the south-east of the promenade . . .* [*reads the Greensward text*], *it is proposed to form a lake of irregular shape, and with an area of eight or nine acres. This arrangement has been suggested by the present nature of the ground, which is low and somewhat swampy. It is conceived that, by introducing such an ornamental sheet of water into the composition at this point, the picturesque effect of the bold bluffs that will run down to its edge and overhang it, must be much increased; and that by means of such a natural boundary, this rocky section of the park will be rendered more retired and attractive as a pleasant walk or lounge.*

The proposed design was not followed altogether. For one thing, the actual acreage of the Pond, when completed, was five acres, and only on the western side of the lower half were there bluffs. Water for the Pond came from DeVoor's Mill Stream, which flowed through the park and emptied into the East River at Turtle Bay. (During a drought the two pools outside the Corning Glass Building, Fifth Avenue and 56th Street, can be filled in part by water from a branch of the stream, still flowing beneath the skyscraper's subbasement.)

A swan boat on the Pond. *Harper's Weekly.*

Museum of the City of New York.

Swan boats, similar to those still in the Boston Garden, used to paddle about the Pond, underscoring the note of quiet and repose as well as the picturesque effect. They plied the waters until 1924, and their passing may be said to have started the destruction of the area. The sacrifice of the bridle path came in 1934, and in 1951 the Wollman Memorial Skating Rink opened. A foundation provided $600,000, and, as often happens, the city had to come forward with an additional amount, this time $400,000. Two of the five acres of water disappeared, and one of the loveliest spots of the park was lost.

> *Of all the effects in landscape* [*wrote Uvedale Price, one of the most influential of eighteenth-century English landscapers*], *the most brilliant and captivating are those produced by water. . . . One striking property of water, and that which most distinguishes it from the grosser element of earth, is its being a mirror; and a mirror which gives a peculiar freshness and tenderness to the colours it reflects: it softens the stronger lights, though the lucid veil it throws over them seems hardly to diminish their brilliancy; and gives breadth, and often depth, to the shadows, while from its glassy surface they gain a peculiar look of transparency.*

Instead of a mirror, there is now a large expanse of concrete, surrounded by hurricane-wire fencing and dotted by unattractive lamp standards. A public-address system bawls music. An artificial skating rink could more properly have been placed off Columbus Circle, where two subway stations make possible convenient transportation. Now that the rink's building is here, it could, at least, be screened by vines, much as the Arsenal is.

The tour takes the path along the former western embankment of the Pond and turns left up the hill past a handsome rare purple-leafed European beech (*Fagus sylvatica* var. *purpurea*). Fenced in on the south is a Bird Sanctuary, established in the 1930's; periodically, there are reports of stray cats molesting the birds, and so far no one has thought of a permanent solution to this menace. If the promenader would find a bench here, he might contrast view before him with the aim of Olmsted and Vaux as it is seen through the eyes of Harold A. Caparn.

> *When conditions are at their best, after rainy weather or in the early morning or evening* [*wrote the landscape architect who laid out the Brooklyn Botanic Garden*], *there is a wonderful air of calm beauty pervading it all, so that one marvels more and more that such a thing with such a sentiment should exist in New York City. . . . Each successive part into which the uneven surface naturally resolves itself is treated according to its own suggestion, with thoroughness and reserve. Buildings and other subordinate objects are carefully set where they will do least harm to the general composition. The ragged countryside planting is arranged in groups or masses or borders with due regard to the habit of the trees, texture, and color of foliage, sky-line and so on. For the rough or divided surface of land is substituted the smooth and continuous lawn, displaying the best contours of the ground, and preserving them unbroken to their logical end. In fact, an informal park is mostly constructed of endless variants of these two features of lawn and planting, of open spaces surrounded by covered ones, as a room or a building is composed of voids and solids.*

Going to the Gapstow Bridge, the promenader can see the contrasting elements on the east and west sides of what remains of the Pond. The view here—the reflection of the towers in the mirror below, seen here a thousand times over—is magnificent. A quick glance north is enough to drive home what has been lost.

On leaving the bridge the promenader will notice, on either side, two lovely, small trees with numerous small leaves. They are silk trees (*Albizzia Julibrissin*); in summer and later into the fall they have bright pink, crown-shaped blossoms. Beyond on the right is a southern catalpa and at the head of the path, a large English elm. The tour goes to the right, following

Looking south from above the yet-unbuilt Gapstow Bridge in 1862. The Bird Sanctuary covers Promontory Rock on the right. St. Luke's Hospital at 55th and 54th streets on the west side of Fifth Avenue is in the middle distance, the Catholic Orphan Asylum at 52nd Street on the east side of the avenue is beyond to the left.

Photo Victor Prevost. Stuart Collection, New York Public Library.

the upper path above the Pond. Numerous pin oaks and black locusts (*Robinia pseudoacacia*) line the route.

Below, along the Pond, is a new wide path of asphalt spread on rock at the water's edge. Formerly lawn went down the embankment, but the ground, trampled by skaters in winter, became mud in spring and dust in summer. It was recommended in 1927 that boulders be placed here in an "artistic manner" with ground-covering vines. The present solution does not even follow this advice.

The few swans in the Pond are the last to remain in the park. They were once found on all the major bodies of water. The first swans appeared in 1860, a gift to Central Park from the City of Hamburg. (Nine of the original twelve died of apoplexy—not of poisoning as many suspected—and were quickly replaced by swans presented by the Royal Companies of Vintners and Dyers of London.) Birds are very much a part of the park's tradition. On part of the site of the Metropolitan Museum of Art, a Dovecot was built in the 1860's. It contained two elaborate wooden birdhouses, designed by Vaux for the pleasure of many varieties of pigeon. Sparrows, too, were once given preferred treatment, for the English sparrow made his American debut in the park. Seven pairs, imported from Europe, were set loose here in 1864. The park's policemen, who wore gray uniforms, were often referred to in the last century as "The Sparrow Cops," their disparagers claiming they had nothing better to do than chase sparrows off the lawns.

Continuing to the large rock at the end of the Pond, the promenader comes to the spot where a chain-grocery heir wished to build a café. The proposal, first suggested in 1959, was turned down by the Lindsay administration, and the park spared another encroachment.

Even in its first decade, the park faced severe threats, and the 1873 *Annual Report of Central Park* attempted to define the issue:

> *But the preparation and preservation of the best possible landscape effects will always depend on a series of conditions of a subtle and delicate character, that are much more liable to be interfered with and encroached upon. If a park, as a whole, is to be considered as a work of art, it is in this direction, then, that it most needs to be carefully protected; for the demands of special art of which it is an example must always have the first claim to consideration. The essence of the park, that is to say, must be in its landscapes. If, as the years elapse, the pictorial effects prove to be as broad, well-marked and varied as was possible under the circumstances of the site, a corresponding measure of*

Central Park in 1864. *J. Clarence Davies Collection, Museum of the City of New York.*

success is assured. . . . The Central Park labors under marked disadvantages in this respect. Its actual dimensions in acres do not seem small, but the spaces of turf or water that have to be depended on to establish the required impression of indefinite extent and comparatively open landscape, are very contracted.

"Considered as a work of art"! Olmsted and Vaux always considered it one. Never a philosopher's garden, like the formal Versailles, but always the picturesque landscape of the emotional man, as Christopher Tunnard has observed, Central Park symbolized the search for the nineteenth-century ideal in visible form. *For all the people*, that was the aim of the designers, and surely that goal was achieved for the first time on a large scale.

On leaving the park proper the promenader stands before the equestrian statue of William Tecumseh Sherman. It will be recalled that the sculptor Augustus Saint-Gaudens and the architect Charles Follen McKim first tried to place this monument at the foot of the Mall, only to meet head-on opposition from Samuel Parsons. As it turned out, the Grand Army Plaza proved a far better site. The statue was dedicated on Decoration Day, 1903.

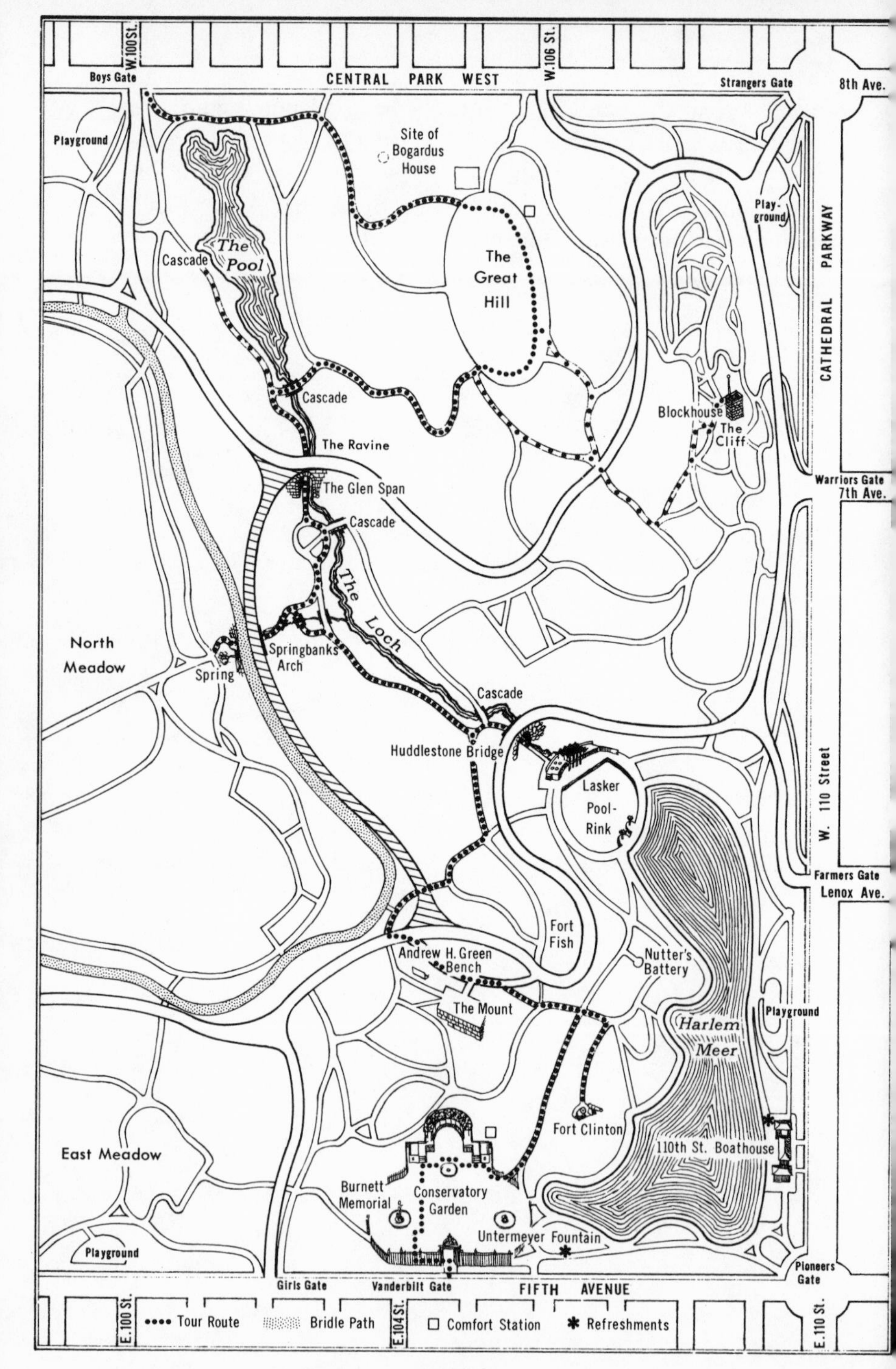
W. 100 St.
W. 106 St.
Boys Gate
CENTRAL PARK WEST
Strangers Gate
8th Ave.
Playground
Site of Bogardus House
Play-ground
CATHEDRAL PARKWAY
The Pool
Cascade
The Great Hill
Cascade
Blockhouse
The Cliff
The Ravine
The Glen Span
Warriors Gate
7th Ave.
Cascade
The Loch
North Meadow
Spring
Springbanks Arch
Cascade
Huddlestone Bridge
Lasker Pool-Rink
W. 110 Street
Farmers Gate
Lenox Ave.
Fort Fish
Andrew H. Green Bench
Nutter's Battery
The Mount
Harlem Meer
Playground
Fort Clinton
East Meadow
110th St. Boathouse
Burnett Memorial
Conservatory Garden
Untermeyer Fountain
Playground
Pioneers Gate
Girls Gate
Vanderbilt Gate
FIFTH AVENUE
E. 100 St.
Tour Route
Bridle Path
E. 104 St.
Comfort Station
Refreshments
E. 110 St.

Tour II

III

WALKING TOUR OF THE NORTHERN SECTION

Transportation: For 100th Street and Central Park West: 96th or 103rd Street Stations of IND Subway; 8th Avenue Bus Line.

The Upper or Northern Section of the park (more particularly the area north of the Reservoir) provides a felicitous contrast to the Southern Section, below the 79th Street Transverse Road. Where the dominating note of the latter is pastoral, the former is predominantly "natural." Steep hills, profusion of rock, thick woods, and three bodies of water linked by a cascading brook join to form a wilderness pleasing to devotees of the picturesque. This Northern Section also differs strikingly from the Southern in another way; "improvements" of recent years have been kept to a minimum. There are intruders on the Greensward plan—permanent tennis courts with a tennis house, a Recreation Center and permanent baseball diamonds with hurricane-wire fencing—but so far aggressive philanthropy has found only one outlet, a modernistic pool-skating rink.

The tour starts at the Pool, just north of the Boys Gate at Central Park West and 100th Street, goes up the Great Hill, and then takes a diversion to the Blockhouse. Returning to the Pool it follows the brook to the Harlem Meer, making a side trip to view the North Meadow. At the end of the waterway the tour climbs the hill where Fort Fish stood in 1814, crosses the East Drive to the Andrew Haswell Green Bench and goes northeast to the site of Fort Clinton. From this point it descends to the Conservatory Garden to exit at the Vanderbilt Gate, Fifth Avenue and 105th Street.

On entering the park at the Boys Gate, Central Park West and 100th Street, the promenader takes the path to the north, which goes down steps. Immediately to the left is a large Osage orange (*Maclura pomifera*) with several more beyond it, easily recognizable by their orange bark. Most of the other trees are black locust (*Robinia pseudoacacia*) with deeply ridged bark. The large tree to the right of the steps is a sycamore maple (*Acer pseudoplatanus*). The path drops rapidly, almost thirty feet, to come to the Pool. Here is an illustration of Olmsted and Vaux's skill in adapting existing terrain to exclude the city's façades; the steep slope to the west, in addition to the fine trees, provides a substantial natural screen.

The slope's height here is due to the cut-and-fill practice of street grading, standard in New York. The hills were "cut" and the hollows "filled" until the bumpy surface of Manhattan all but disappeared save in the parks. All around the park, as early photographs show, the street grades were lowered or raised as much as twenty feet, in this instance even more. As the grading in this part of the city took place relatively late, around the 1870's, when large parcels of the West Side were thrown on the market and sold at auction, the park's wall was not completed until the 1880's. The foundation of the wall, much in evidence here, is schist, some of it from the park; the base stone, level with the sidewalk, is mountain graywacke and the upper wall, yellow freestone (now begrimed) from New Brunswick, Nova Scotia.

The Pool was formed from a stream, Montayne's Rivulet, which originated in the old days at Columbus Avenue and 95th Street, flowed into the park at the foot of the incline, continuing down to what is now Harlem Meer and emptied into Harlem Creek at Fifth Avenue and 107th Street. A stream of some size, Harlem Creek flowed into the East River. The tour follows in part the present landscaped course of the old rivulet, whose name stemmed from that of a Walloon family, de la Montayne, who owned a farm nearby. In the 1880's the

Pool had a planting of water lily and lotus. Today the Pool's banks are trampled, part of the abuse the park suffers. The contour of the Pool has undergone a number of changes over the years during the removal of silt, cleaning, and repairing of the banks. As late as the 1930's a small island existed off the north bank.

Standing between the Pool and the path is a fine bald cypress (*Taxodium distichum*) with fuzzy orange bark and small yellow-green leaves. To the west of the path are a number of tulip trees (*Liriodendron tulipifera*), identified by their tall trunks with reddish-tinged bark. Looking east across the Pool the promenader can make out the Glen Span, carrying the West Drive across the Ravine.

Leaving the Pool, the tour takes the left fork up the Great Hill and passes by the 103rd Street park entrance, nameless since it was not one of the original gates, given their names in 1862. Coming to the top of the Great Hill or Bogardus Hill, the promenader will notice a slight rise directly west of the path, at lamppost No. 0341. This rise is 134 feet high, the third highest site in the park, coming after Vista Rock, site of Belvedere Castle (135 feet) and Summit Rock, in line with 83rd Street at Central Park West (137 feet, six inches). The Bogardus House, predating the park, stood on this rise for many years. When he was daily working on the park Olmsted resided in the house, and it was here that he married his brother John's widow in 1859. In the 1890's the Park Department ordered the house torn down after deciding the cost of converting it to a comfort station would be excessive. On the Great Hill the park's designers considered placing a tower, and later, an observatory. In the park's early days the hill commanded a splendid view of the Hudson and East rivers, as neither planting nor building obscured the horizon. For a long time it was a favorite picnic ground, a spur of the West Drive circuiting the hilltop.

The ambience has changed considerably since the turn of

the century when the whole of the hilltop, other than the graveled drive, was given over to lawn and trees. Small croquet grounds with timbered curbing and flower beds as a western border were placed here in the 1920's, but the desolate look of the spot is fairly recent. On the left is a large asphalt apron with hurricane-wire fencing originally designed for horseshoe pitching. On the right is a curious amalgam of asphalt and concrete with its chief ornament a pair of large sandlots called croquet grounds. Examining it more carefully the visitor will remark first a wide band of asphalt, next a narrower band of Belgian block happily being carpeted by grass, third a wide band of concrete, formerly part of the graveled drive and, last, the sandlots with an asphalt apron for shuffleboard at the eastern end. What the promenader beholds is a typical example of how park policy of the last decades answered public needs only in terms of asphalt and recreation equipment. At least in the matter of planting there is some consolation: nearly all the trees are still American elms.

At the Great Hill the promenader has a choice—either to continue around the croquet grounds and down a path on the eastern slope of the hill to the Pool, or to take the path at the northeast corner for a side tour to visit an ancient blockhouse.

If he chooses the latter, the promenader follows what was once part of the drive, now happily reduced to a path. The route crosses the West Drive and continues bearing left past elm, oak, maple, beech, black cherry and ironwood. Where the path turns sharply left, at lamppost No. 0717, there are two large tulip trees. At a high outcrop of rock on the right, part of an elevation called "The Cliff," there stands a square stone box. Taking the crude path up the rock, with its glacial marking, the promenader goes left and finds himself in front of Blockhouse No. 1, one of four built during the War of 1812. In the first two years of the war nothing was done to protect the city on its land side, but with the threat of British invasion in the early part of 1814, it was obvious that some steps had to be taken. The enemy bombardment of Stonington, Connecticut, on August tenth roused New Yorkers to build a chain of forts running from Third Avenue and 106th Street west and north to Harlem Heights above 125th Street and the Hudson. Blockhouse No. 1 originally had a sunken roof on which was placed a cannon *en barbette*, meaning one so mounted that it could fire in any direction over a parapet. Fortunately the Blockhouse was never put to the test.

In 1858 the park's northern boundary stopped at 106th Street, as seen in the Greensward plan. Looking down from the Cliff, it is obvious why the Park Commissioners decided in 1859 to extend the boundary to 110th Street. The additional area seemed a natural part of the park, and the cost of grading the rocky hills at 106th Street would have been formidable. The sixty-five acres were acquired by 1863, and their cost reflects the park's success. What in 1860 had been appraised at $183,850 cost the city $1,179,590. In 1856 park land had cost $8,121 an acre; in 1863, the cost per acre north of 106th Street was about $18,147.

A brook, cascade, and small pool about three hundred feet due east of Blockhouse No. 1, long neglected, were restored in 1967, and the banks planted with azalea and rhododendron.

The tour returns to the West Drive by the same route it took to the Blockhouse. The paths in this part of the park, incidentally, were of cinders in the early 1930's; other than being cheap, cinders had the advantage of providing a porous surface, whereas asphalt invites erosion. Across the West Drive the path leads south via the Great Hill, turning due south at lamppost No. 0539, and descends gradually to the Pool. The tour crosses a bridge formerly embellished with rustic railings at the foot of the Pool. The curious may continue along the Pool's south border to a small cascade. Here, in the course of the primary campaign of 1965, when the water shortage was very much an issue, one of the Democratic candidates discovered that the flow, unusually abundant despite the drought, was due to a leaking main. The leak was stopped much to the grief of the Park Department men who knew about the leak all along but were grateful to have at least one source of water.

The tour takes the path near the wooden bridge at the foot of the Pool to enter the Ravine via the Glen Span. The walk now parallels the Brook and the two continue under and beyond the span. After passing through the arch, the promenader can turn back to glimpse the cascade; this, in palmier days, was one of the sights of the park.

Continuing east, the tour goes through a very picturesque setting, completely cut off from the city. Another bridge, today the simplest kind, for it has lost its railing of red cedar, crosses the brook, but instead of taking it, the tour goes right and right again at the creek descending from the south. Following the creek the promenader comes to the low Springbanks Arch, carrying the bridle path and an abandoned portion of the drive over the walk. In the old days a sign posting the park regulations was set in a rustic frame and stood to one side of the arch; these signs were standard throughout the park.

"All persons are forbidden—" the sign announced:

To enter or leave the Park except by the gateways.

To climb or walk upon the wall.

To turn cattle, horses, goats, or swine into the Park.

To carry firearms or to throw stones or other missiles within it, etc.

Park visitors were also warned:

No threatening, abusive, insulting, or indecent language shall be allowed on the Central Park, whereby a breach of peace may be occasioned.

The Springbanks Arch at the North Meadow, c. 1870. The rustic frame on the right holds a slate tablet inscribed with the park rules; this was one of many placed around the Park in the early days.

New-York Historical Society.

No person shall be allowed to tell fortunes or play at any game of chance at, or with any table or instrument of gaming, nor to do any obscene or indecent act whatever on the Central Park.

No person shall fire, discharge, or set off in the Central Park, any rocket, cracker, torpedo, squib, balloon, snake, chaser, or double-header, nor any fireworks. . . .

Continuing through Springbanks Arch, the promenader goes up some steps and finds himself on the edge of the North Meadow. With its baseball diamonds and hurricane-wire fencing it is one of the more active sports grounds in the park. A description of the North Meadow in the early 1890's illustrates how changing fashion has influenced park use.

The sheen of the grass, the varied tints of the foliage sweeping the turf to the left, the low-lying hillocks crowned with large forest trees, the great boulders entirely exposed or only half submerged, the meadow beyond running back to seemingly unknown distances—who will picture it truly? [exclaimed *Superintendent of Parks Samuel Parsons in 1891*]. *There is dignity, there is breadth, repose, restfulness, and yet a sense of isolation that is not absolute. It is genuine park scenery that the eye is tempted to linger on and the foot to walk on, and presents, if viewed as a single feature, one of the best examples we have of good park work.*

In those days the meadow, the largest one in the park, was thickly carpeted with Kentucky Blue Grass, replaced today by a mixture of NK-100 Perennial Rye, a hardy, quick germinator, and Fescue (like a dry martini, four to one). The meadow takes a hard beating as football follows baseball and the athletes wear cleats, formerly forbidden. Despite the use, the turf stands up surprisingly well when aerified, watered and limed. During Olmsted and Vaux's time, adults were not allowed to play baseball in the park. At that time, the park was not seen as the proper place for active recreationists. The first baseball diamonds appeared in the North Meadow in the 1920's, the present number with the extensive fencing belong to the 1930's era and have destroyed the original concept of an unbroken stretch of pastoral meadow. Hurricane-wire fencing, particularly in quantity, blights the landscape. Perhaps in the near future the metal fencing will be replaced by a strong plastic, light enough to be a temporary installation. Lawn tennis was permitted here in the past, as it was on the Sheep Meadow, employing temporary netting and posts; the coming of equipment recreation brought permanent courts, which today are to the southwest of the North Meadow, along with a tennis house.

The promenader may be surprised to learn that until the 1930's no asphalt walks crossed the meadow north-south at this point; their absence explains why the turf had such a sweep in the 1890's. This fine vista, however, was not always fully appreciated; the North Meadow was proposed in 1881, and again in 1889, as a fitting site for the World's Fair. This was due, in part, to the relatively little use the Northern Section of the park received until the present century with the northward move of population. The landscaping of this section progressed slowly, and there were still unlandscaped portions during the first decades of this century.

The building directly to the south was formerly the Farm Building; in the 1930's it was converted into a Recreation Building, chiefly for old men. Handball courts adjoin it on the north. The structure is very badly sited and designed, wholly out of keeping with the Olmsted and Vaux ideal.

On retracing his steps to the Springbanks Arch, the promenader will notice on his right a small crevice with rockwork, out of which in rainy weather water flows running down to the creek. The tour goes back through the arch and crosses to the creek's right side. The juncture of the creek and brook, now swampy ground, once marked the western end of the Loch, a narrow pond. Due to the departmental policy of allowing silt to accumulate, the Loch disappeared in recent decades. As sad as the little stream is along here, hopeful youngsters poke around trying to find crawfish.

To the right a meadow with weeping willow and birch sweeps down to the former Loch. On the opposite bank rises the forest, making this one of the most surprising and delightful landscapes of Central Park.

At the end of what the Park Department map (and the authors') hopefully calls the Loch—a more appropriate name would be "the Trickle"—is another cascade, so much a part of this valley. Beyond it is the Huddlestone Bridge carrying the East Drive over path and brook. Through the arch the promenader can make out the Loula D. Lasker Pool-Rink, the latest of the philanthropic "improvements" in the park. The Loula D. Lasker Foundation offered $500,000 in 1961 for construction of a rink, with the city to match the sum. By 1966 the cost had risen to $3,500,000; the Foundation's gift rose only to $604,420. The "pool," it should be noted, is only four feet deep. The site was, in any case, recklessly chosen as it is almost impossible to provide adequate drainage here. Even before it opened, the building was flooded by a downpour, and the resulting damage to machinery cost over $250,000 to repair. The Department must not be blamed for the grotesque intrusion. Such was the pressure brought on Mayor Wagner by the Foundation that he overruled Commissioner Morris's strong opposition. Ironically, while the pool-rink was being built, Olmsted and Vaux's park was disappearing.

The tour leaves what was the Loch at lamppost No. 0554 to take the walk going sharply up the hill, at the top of which a spur juts north. In the War of 1812 this was the site of Fort

Cascade south of Huddlestone Bridge. *Photo Katrina Thomas.*

Fish, named for Nicholas Fish, Chairman of the Committee of Defense. The walk continues to the abandoned cross-drive. If the asphalt strip were removed, green acres would be gained

A sunny afternoon on the bridle path. The Chinese Fleece Vine, to the left, gives a splash of white to the scene. *Photo John Albok.*

and, more, a fine sweep of lawn. The galvanized-iron lamps, which have no place in the park, could then also be ripped out. Just beyond this strip is the familiar bridle path, bridged here, in the park's early days, by two arbors that must have provided a charming sight for beholder as well as rider.

The tour crosses the East Drive to follow an old driveway of imitation Belgian blocks. Just east of the latter stands a lonely marble bench, a memorial to Andrew Haswell Green, 1820-1903. Five American elms, symbolizing the five boroughs (mentioned on the bench's inscription) once grew nearby but all fell victim to Dutch elm disease.

Green's name figures prominently in the park's history, for he was elected Treasurer of the Board of Park Commissioners in 1857. His name also figures prominently in the city's history. He worked to expand the public school system and to establish public parks and championed municipal reform during and after the Tweed Regime. He helped to organize the American Museum of Natural History and the Metropolitan Museum of Art and to locate the New York Zoological Society in the Bronx. As trustee of the estate of his law partner, Samuel J. Tilden, he had a key role in the founding of the New York Public Library. Largely thanks to him, the words "Tilden Foundation" are inscribed on the frieze of the 42nd Street building along with "Astor Library" and "Lenox Library." Together with Olmsted, Charles Eliot Norton and others, he saved Niagara Falls from commercial exploitation. Landmarks preservation owes him honor as founder of the American Scenic and Historic Preservation Society. Above all, he led the campaign to establish Greater New York, a vision he had as early as 1868. In 1890 he was made head of the commission organized by the State Legislature to look into the question of municipal consolidation, i.e., of old New York, Brooklyn and neighboring towns. (One of the commission's members was Calvert Vaux.) When, in 1896, a charter commission was appointed to draw up a charter for Greater New York, Green was its president. No wonder that, after January 1, 1898, with the coming of the metropolis, Andrew Haswell Green was hailed as "Father of Greater New York." Such was the man who served the city "whose glory," as he put it, "is our pride." He was killed at the age of eighty-one by an insane man who mistook him for someone else.

Green's bench is on the site of the original McGown's Tavern kept by the McGown family in the eighteenth century and the early part of the nineteenth. The family also left their name to McGown's Pass, the dip where the East Drive drops to turn west; the Old Post Road, not closed within the park until 1859, followed the route of the present drive along here. On September 15, 1776, in this part of the city, a Maryland regiment under Colonel William Smallwood succeeded in delaying the British invaders, an action that allowed General Washington to assemble his retreating forces on Harlem Heights. The Marylanders, outflanked, pulled back during the night of the fifteenth to join the General and eventually abandoned the island after the Battle of Manhattan. McGown's Pass and Tavern then became part of the enemy's defenses.

The McGowns held the property until 1845. Two years later it passed into the hands of the Sisters of Charity of St. Vincent de Paul. The tavern was transformed and enlarged, a small complex of buildings was added, and the Academy and Convent of St. Vincent established, the site being renamed Mount St. Vincent. A new wing of the institution stood on the platform at present occupied by the park's large mulch pile. In 1856 the property was taken for park land. Two years later the Sisters moved to the estate of the actor Edwin Forrest in Riverdale, "Fonthill," where today the convent and school thrive as the College of Mount St. Vincent-on-the-Hudson. Olmsted and his bride lived in the main building for a short time after leaving the Bogardus House. During the Civil War, it was used as a soldiers' hospital. In 1866 the main building reverted to its former status, a tavern, run by a popular restaurateur, Colonel Stetson. The chapel was transformed into a statuary hall and filled with plaster casts of the work of Thomas Crawford, sculptor of the bronze doors of the National Capitol as well as of the "Armed Liberty" on top of the Capitol dome. Other buildings of Mount St. Vincent accommodated members of the Park Department staff for a time. A fire burned Mount St. Vincent to the ground in 1881.

The Mount Saint Vincent Convent buildings which had been converted to a tavern, park offices and a statuary hall. They burned to the ground in 1881. *Museum of the City of New York.*

Crawford's statues were rescued, but no one today knows where they are. Two years later another tavern was built on the site and given the name of McGown's Pass Tavern. There was public protest, people objecting to another building in their park. At the request of the Sisters of Charity the official name of the site was changed from Mount St. Vincent to McGown's Pass. The new tavern initiated the pleasant custom of offering a bottle of fine wine to the first sleigh to reach the tavern with the season's first snow. The building lasted until 1917, when it was torn down by Mayor John Purroy

Mitchel; reforming mayors seem to have an antipathy for park restaurants, *vide* Mayor La Guardia and the destruction of the old Casino.

The tour follows the path going along the East Drive, takes the fork to the right and goes left at lamppost No. 0616. On the right of the path going up the knoll is a clump of Japanese black pine (*Pinus thunbergi*). The promenader now finds himself on a platform whose chief ornaments (other than a large horse chestnut) are a cannon and a mortar. A plaque tells the story of the site's occupation by the British in the Revolutionary War and its later history. Here was built on August 13, 1814, a small fort, Fort Clinton, named for Mayor De Witt Clinton, part of the line of defense mentioned already in connection with Blockhouse No. 1. Among those who volunteered to build the ramparts in 1814 were members of the Society of Saint Tammany, Columbia College students, the tallow chandlers, and a squad of master butchers who arrived with a banner reading:

> Friends of Our Country
> Free Trade and Butchers' Rights
> From Brooklyn's Fields to Harlem Heights

Fort Clinton was linked to Nutter's Battery, which stood to the northwest on the other side of McGown's Pass. Some 1,600 men of the State Militia manned the fortifications from here to Harlem Heights. By December of 1814, rumors of peace leaked from Europe, and many militiamen, their three-month term up, were mustered out. On February 11, 1815, the news arrived that a peace treaty ending the War of 1812 had been signed at Ghent; the defenses in the city were abandoned for good.

Below the hill lies Harlem Meer. The opportunity to add this large basin of water influenced the decision to acquire the land from 106th to 110th streets. The Meer, completed in

1866, had for years a turf bank and was noted for its "sylvan setting." A jet of water once played in the center. The present rim of concrete and asphalt was constructed in the 1940's. Latin-American concerts are currently presented on summer evenings near the boathouse.

The promenader abandons the site of Fort Clinton and goes down the hill to the Conservatory Garden. The foundations built into the hill on the right date back to Mount St. Vincent. Even in the Greensward plan, this part of the park was set aside for special planting. Olmsted and Vaux planned a large aboretum of native trees and shrubs. This proved unfeasible, but a nursery was established here, next, a few greenhouses and finally in 1899, an elaborate Conservatory was built, featuring lavish seasonal displays. It was torn down in 1934. Prospect Park lost its Conservatory in 1947. The disappearance of the two reflected a general disregard for planting noticeable throughout the city's park system.

The present formal garden was designed by Thomas D. Price in 1936. There are two pieces of sculpture: to the north, the Untermeyer Fountain, 1947, by Walter Schott; to the south, the Frances Hodgson Burnett Memorial, 1936, by Bessie Potter Vonnoh. Borders of flowering quince, wichura rose and English yew predominate in the garden. Some beds have arabesques of gray-green telenthera mixed with seasonal planting. Magnolia and crab apples provide added color in the spring. On the hillside is a wrought-iron arbor with Chinese wisteria, splendid in late May. The symmetrical paths and the carefully tended planting are in sharp contrast to the picturesque, "natural" park.

These two tours, the Northern and Southern, serve only to introduce the park. Every visitor has his own favorite tour, just as he has his own favorite view. Central Park, like any great work of art, always offers fresh surprises and quickens new interest and new delight.

The tour leaves the park by the Vanderbilt Gate. Formerly at the Cornelius Vanderbilt II mansion, which occupied the site of Bergdorf Goodman between 57th and 58th streets on Fifth Avenue, the gate was given to the city in 1939 by Mrs. Gertrude Vanderbilt Whitney, founder of the Whitney Museum of American Art. It was made in Paris by Bergrotte and Bauviller.

Nearby, at 104th Street, is the Museum of the City of New York. Historical material on Central Park has been placed on permanent loan at the museum by the Department of Parks. An original Greensward design for a section of the park is usually on view.

APPENDIX A

Other Points of Interest

The Arsenal, built by the state in 1848, housed troops during the Civil War. Past tenants include the American Museum of Natural History, the Zoo and the Weather Observatory. The current occupant, the Department of Parks, moved out briefly from 1914 to 1924 to take up quarters in the Municipal Building. In 1915 it was announced that the building, considered an eyesore, would be pulled down. The Arsenal remained standing, and a lease was granted in 1918 for its use as an American Museum of Safety. Some citizens felt this proposal was so ridiculous that they took the city to court, and the lease was canceled. The front stairs, with an unusual railing of rifles, lead to an entrance hall with murals of park scenes and maps painted by Allen Saalburg in 1935. The original Greensward plan is displayed in the third-floor hall.

Lion's Head Rock is the name of the large outcrop overhanging the south edge of the drive in line with 109th Street, midway between Central Park West and Seventh Avenue.

The Obelisk, west of the East Drive in line with 81st Street, was built in 1600 B.C. by King Thotmes III. It stood in front of the Temple of the Sun at Heliopolis, Egypt, until the Romans removed it to Alexandria in 12 B.C. and placed it before a temple built by Cleopatra. For very little reason it is sometimes referred to as "Cleopatra's Needle." The Khedive of Egypt offered it to New Yorkers in 1877, William H. Vanderbilt financed the transportation cost, and the Obelisk was erected in the park in 1881. Despite special protective coatings, the rose-red granite from Nubia has been weathered badly by city grime. A twin to New York's Obelisk stands on the Embankment of the Thames in London. The plaques translating the hieroglyphs were presented by Cecil B. de Mille.

The Shakespeare Garden, to the west of Belvedere Castle, started off as the "Garden of the Heart." In 1915, a year after its completion, it was taken over by the Shakespeare Society and changed identity. Cuttings from Stratford-on-Avon were planted, but only a black mulberry survives. The garden is supposed to contain plants and shrubs named in the Bard's work.

The Swedish Schoolhouse, below the Shakespeare Garden, is a replica made in Sweden for the Philadelphia Exposition and moved to the park in 1876. It now serves as headquarters for the Marionette Theater of the Department of Parks.

Summit Rock, in line with 83rd Street and Central Park West, is the highest elevation in the park—137½ feet. A spur of the West Drive used to circuit the hilltop, and in the center where there is now a sand pit stood the statue of Simón Bolívar, before its removal to 59th Street and Sixth Avenue. The hotel directly across the way on Central Park West still bears the name of the great South American liberator.

APPENDIX B

Recreation and Other Events Offered in Central Park

Sports

Sport and/or Facility	*No.*	*Location*
Baseball Diamonds permit required	8	North Meadow; bleacher seats adjoin diamonds
Bicycle Paths A bicycle concession is located at the 72nd Street Boathouse.	3	From 72nd Street and West Drive south to 59th Street, east to East Drive, north on East Drive to 72nd Street—2.5 miles
Bicycling on drives when park is closed to traffic		104th Street Crossroad—.25 miles North end of old Center Drive, open to bicyclists from November 1st to April 1st—.38 miles
Boating fee	2	The Lake, 72nd Street Boathouse, 300 rowboats Harlem Meer, 100 rowboats
Bowling Greens permit required	2	Sheep Meadow, 67th Street near West Drive
Bridle Path		See end map for route, 4.5 miles

Sport and/or Facility	*No.*	*Location*
Coasting Areas	6	Burns Lawn, 79th Street and West Drive south of Transverse Road
		Cedar Hill, 79th Street and East Drive
		East Meadow, 99th Street off Fifth Avenue
		Pilgrim Hill, 72nd Street and East Drive
		60th Street and West Drive, near Heckscher Playground
		79th Street and East Drive (short run for small children)
Croquet	2	Great Hill, 105th Street west
Fishing		The Lake, for children sixteen and under, April to November
Football Field	1	North Meadow
Handball	1	North Meadow Playground, 97th Street
Hockey Fields	2	Great Lawn
		Sheep Meadow, for children twelve years and under
Horseshoe Pitching	9	Heckscher Playground
	5	Great Lawn
	5	North Meadow
Ice Skating on Outdoor Artificial Rinks	2	Wollman Memorial Rink
fee		Lasker Pool-Rink
Model Yachting		Conservatory Water, storage facilities available at Kerbs Boathouse
Paddle Tennis	1	Heckscher Playground
	3	North Meadow
Pony Track fee		Central Park Zoo Area, 64th Street and Fifth Avenue
Roller Skating		The Mall
Shuffleboard		Great Hill
Skiing		Burns Lawn, West Drive at 79th Street
		Cedar Hill, East Drive at 79th Street

Sport and/or Facility	*No.*	*Location*
Soccer Fields	1	Great Lawn
	3	North Meadow
Softball Diamonds	8	Great Lawn
permit required	4	North Meadow
	6	Heckscher Playground
Swimming Pool 4 feet deep		Lasker Pool-Rink
Tennis Courts permit required	30	93rd Street and West Drive
Wading Pools	3	Heckscher Playground
		Northwest Playground, 85th Street east of West Drive
		Wollman Playground, opposite 63rd Street

Sports permits are issued at the Arsenal.

Other Events

Carousel fee	Friedsam Memorial Carousel, opposite 65th Street in center of park
Chess and Checkers House equipment provided gratis	Opposite 64th Street in center of park on Kinderberg
Children's Zoo fee	Between 65th and 66th streets, adjoining Fifth Avenue
Concerts, marionette shows and other entertainments are presented in various parts of the park throughout the summer; for program information apply to the Department of Parks, the Arsenal, Central Park, New York 10021.	Mall Sheep Meadow Harlem Meer Wollman Memorial Rink
Shakespeare Festival Company presents plays of Shakespeare no admission charge	Delacorte Theatre below Belvedere Castle

Storytelling sponsored by the New York Public Library on Saturday mornings during the summer	Hans Christian Andersen statue, just west of Conservatory Water
Zoo	64th Street and Fifth Avenue

(Over two hundred special events take place in the park yearly, ranging from school field days and bicycle races to "happenings," poetry readings and wreath layings.)

Refreshments

Restaurants: Tavern-on-the-Green, 67th Street adjoining Central Park West and the Fountain Café at the Terrace.

Cafeterias: The Zoo, 72nd Street Boathouse and the Metropolitan Museum of Art.

Refreshment Stands: Friedsam Memorial Carousel, Wollman Memorial Rink, Children's Zoo, Concession Building at north end of Sheep Meadow, 72nd Street Boathouse, Kerbs Memorial Model Boathouse at Conservatory Water, Concession Building at 106th Street near Fifth Avenue, Lasker Pool-Rink, and 110th Street Boathouse.

Portable refreshment stands are pushed through the park during warm weather.

APPENDIX C

Approximate Dates of Leafing, Budding, Blossoming and Fruiting of Plants in Central Park, adapted from a list prepared by Cornelius M. O'Shea, Horticulturist, Borough of Manhattan

Tree maps of several sections of the park have been published by the Greensward Foundation. They can be obtained from the Department of Parks.

February 10-20

Narcissus–leaf

March 20-31

Korean Rhododendron—*Rhododendron mucronuletum*—purple-pink flower
Honeysuckle—*Lonicera*—leaf
American Elm—*Ulmus americana*—browish-yellow flower

April 1-10

Peony—*Paeonia*—red leafbuds
American Filbert (Hazel)—*Corylus americana*—gray catkins *

April 10-20

Gray Birch—*Betula populifolia*—catkins
European White Birch—*Betula pendula*—catkins
Cutleaf European Birch—*Betula pendula*, var. *alba gracilis*—catkins
Sweet Birch—*Betula lenta*—catkins
Moss or Mountain Phlox—*Phlox subulata albiflora*—white flowers
Border Forsythia—*Forsythia intermedia*—yellow flower
Cornelian Cherry—*Cornus mas*—yellow flower
Japanese Andromeda—*Pieris japonica*—white flower
Weeping Willow—*Salix babylonica*—leaf
Showy Border Forsythia—*Forsythia intermedia* var. *spectabilis*—bright yellow flower
Weeping Forsythia—*Forsythia suspensa*—yellow flower
Fortune Weeping Forsythia—*Forsythia suspensa* var. *fortunei*—yellow flower
Siebold Weeping Forsythia—*Forsythia suspensa* var. *sieboldi*—yellow flower
Sugar Maple—*Acer saccharum*—flower and leaf
Japanese Maple—*Acer palmatum*—leaf
Yulan Magnolia—*Magnolia denudata*—white flower
European Privet—*Ligustrum vulgare*—leaf

April 20-30

Saucer Magnolia—*Magnolia soulangeana*—pink and white flower
Norway Maple—*Acer platanoides*—green yellow flower
Japanese Barberry—*Berberis thunbergi*—leaf

* Catkin: A spike of flowers growing in the axil of a small leaf

European Hornbeam–*Carpinus betulus*–catkins
Saucer Magnolia (Lennei)–*Magnolia soulangeana lennei*–rosy purple flower
Siberian Pea Tree–*Caragana arborescens*–leaf
Big Scentless Mock Orange–*Philadelphus grandiflorus*–leaf
Ginkgo–*Ginkgo biloba*–leaf
Wintergreen Barberry–*Berberis julianae*–fragrant yellow
Common Flowering Quince–*Chaenomoles lagenaria*–scarlet-red to pink flowers
Japanese Flowering Quince–*Chaenomoles japonica*–orange-scarlet flower
Higan Cherry–*Prunus subhirtella*–pink flower
Weeping Higan Cherry–*Prunus subhirtella* var. *pendula*–pink flower
Flowering Dogwood–*Cornus florida*–white
Highbush Blueberry–*Vaccinium corymbosum*–white pinkish flower
Hawthorn–*Crataegus*–leaf
Tree of Heaven–*Ailanthus altissima*–leaf
European Beech–*Fagus sylvatica*–leaf
Copper or Purple Beech–*Fagus sylvatica* var. *purpurea*–leaf
American Beech–*Fagus grandifolia*–leaf
Oriental Plane Tree–*Platanus orientalis*–leaf
Sycamore–*Platanus occidentalis*–leaf
Hop Hornbeam–*Ostrya virginica*–catkins
Saucer Magnolia (Alexandrina)–*Magnolia soulangeana* var. *alexandrina*–pink and white
American Elm–*Ulmus americana*–leaf and fruit
Slippery Elm–*Ulmus fulva*–leaf and fruit
English Elm–*Ulmus procera*–leaf and fruit
Siberian Elm–*Ulmus pumila*–leaf and fruit
Red Flowering Dogwood–*Cornus florida* var. *rubra*–bright pink flower
Pin Cherry–*Prunus pensylvanica*–white flower
Oriental Cherry–*Prunus serrulata*–double white

May 1-10

White Ash–*Fraxinus americana*–blackish flower clusters
Evergreen Candytuft–*Iberis sempervirens*–white flower
Common Chokecherry–*Prunus virginiana*–white flower
Pinxterbloom Azalea–*Rhododendron nudiflorum*–light pink flower

Japanese Flowering Crab Apple–*Malus floribunda*–pink buds opening white

Halls Crab Apple (Parkman)–*Malus halliana* var. *parkmani*–double bright flower

Sargent Crab Apple–*Malus sargenti*–white flower

Torch Azalea–*Rhododendron obtusum* var. *kaempferi*–*red* flower

Black Jetbead–*Rhodotypos scandens*–white flower

Siberian Pea Tree–*Caragana arborescens*–yellow flower

Sycamore Maple–*Acer pseudoplatanus*–green yellow flower

Carolina Silver Bell–*Halesia carolina*–white bells

Japanese Barberry–*Berberis thunbergi*–yellow flower

Red Leaf Japanese Barberry–*Berberis thunbergi atropurpurea*–reddish purple leaf

Allegany Serviceberry–*Amelanchier laevis*–white flower

Carmine Crab Apple–*Malus atrosanguinea*–deep carmine flower

Carolina Rhododendron–*Rhododendron carolinianum*–rosy pink flower

Chinese Wisteria–*Wisteria sinensis*–blue flower

Thicket Hawthorn–*Crataegus intricata*–red fruit

Common Lilac–*Syringa vulgaris*–flowers varying purple-red and lilac according to varieties

Pinxterbloom Azalea–*Rhododendron nudiflorum* var. *roseum*–rose-pink flower

Common Sassafras–*Sassafras albidum*–greenish yellow flower

Amoena Azalea–*Rhododendron obtusum* var. *amoenum*–double purple flower

Morrow Honeysuckle–*Lonicera morrowi*–small flower tinged with yellow

Tatarian Honeysuckle–*Lonicera tatarica*–pinkish flower, same in varieties *rosea* and *bella*

May 10-20

Caucasian Peashrub–*Caragana grandiflora*–yellow flower

Korean Yodogawa Azalea–*Rhododendron yedoense* var. *poukhanense*–bluish lavender flower

Warty Barberry–*Berberis verruculosa*–yellow flower

Common Hackberry–*Celtis occidentalis*–leaf

Common Lilac–*Syringa vulgaris*–purple flower

White Common Lilac–*Syringa vulgaris* var. *alba*–white flower

Black Haw–*Viburnum prunifolium*–white flower

Kansas Hawthorn–*Crataegus coccinoides*–white flower
Frosted Hawthorn–*Crataegus pruinosa*–white flower
Wayfaring Tree–*Viburnum lantana*–white flower
Lily of the Valley–*Convallaria majalis*–white flower
Horse Chestnut–*Aesculus hippocastanum*–white flower
Bogbice Violet–*Viola cucullata*–blue flower
Doublefile Viburnum–*Viburnum tomentosum*–white flower
Japanese Snowball Viburnum–*Viburnum plicatum* var. *tomentosum*–white flower
Yodogawa Azalea–*Rhododendron yedoense*–double rose lilac flower
Amoena Azalea–*Rhododendron obtusum* var. *amoenum (Hinodegiri)*–brilliant crimson flower
Empress Tree–*Paulownia tomentosa*–blue-purple
European Cranberry Bush–*Viburnum opulus*–white flower
Catawba Rhododendron–*Rhododendron catawbiense*–pink flower
Sungari Redbead Cotoneaster–*Cotoneaster racemiflora* var. *soongarica*–white flower
Snow Azalea–*Rhododendron mucronatum*–white flower
Rhododendron mucronulatum var. *magnifica*–rose-purple flower
German Iris–*Iris germanica*–flower in variety of colors
Red Chokeberry–*Aronia arbutifolia*–white flower tinged red
Rugosa Rose–*Rosa rugosa*–rosy crimson flower
Indica Azalea–*Rhododendron indicum*–salmon red flower
Chinese Azalea–*Rhododendron molle*–reddish orange flower
Weigela Florida–*Weigela amabilis*–pink flower
Weigela Florida–*Weigela rosea*–rose flower
Siebold's Viburnum–*Viburnum sieboldi*–white flower
Red Osier Dogwood–*Cornus stolonifera*–white flower
European Mountain Ash–*Sorbus aucuparia*–white flower

May 20-31

English Hawthorn–*Crataegus oxyacantha*–white flower
Singlepink English Hawthorn–*Crataegus oxyacantha* var. *rosea* –red flower
Nannyberry–*Viburnum lentago*–creamy white flower

Lilac Honeysuckle—*Lonicera syringantha*—rosy lilac flower
White Oak—*Quercus alba*—leaf and flower
Northern Red Oak—*Quercus borealis*—leaf and flower
Scarlet Oak—*Quercus coccinea*—leaf and flower
Black Oak—*Quercus velutina*—leaf and flower
Pin Oak—*Quercus palustris*—leaf and flower
Swamp Chestnut Oak—*Quercus prinus*—leaf and flower
Beauty Bush—*Kolkwitsia amabilis*—light pink flower
Rock Cotoneaster—*Cotoneaster horizontalis*—pink flower
Red Horse Chestnut—*Aesculus carnea*—red flower
Black Cherry—*Prunus serotina*—white racemes *
Persian Lilac—*Syringa persica*—lilac flower
White Persian Lilac—*Syringa persica* var. *alba*—white flower
Mountain Laurel—*Kalmia latifolia*—delicate pink flower
Scarlet Firethorn—*Pyracantha coccinea*—white flower
White Rugosa Rose—*Rosa rugosa* var. *alba*—white flower
Virginalis Mock Orange—*Philadelphus virginalis*—double white fragrant flower
Franchet Cotoneaster—*Cotoneaster francheti*—pinkish racemes
Tulip Tree—*Liriodendron tulipifera*—yellowish green flower
Witherod—*Viburnum cassinoides*—white flower
Cockspur Thorn—*Crataegus crus-galli*—white flower
Black Locust—*Robinia pseudoacacia*—white flower
Oriental Photinia—*Photinia villosa*—white flower
Three-spined Barberry—*Berberis triacanthophora*—white flower
Arrowwood—*Viburnum dentatum*—creamy white flower
Maple-leaf Viburnum—*Viburnum acerifolium*—white flower
Peony—*Paeonia*—flowers in white and pink varieties
Sweet Mock Orange—*Philadelphus coronarius*—fragrant white flower
Amur Cork Tree—*Phellodendron amurense*—greenish flower
Sweetbay Magnolia—*Magnolia virginiana (glauca)*—white
Eastern Burning Bush—*Euonymus atropurpureus*—greenish flower
Japanese Snowbell—*Styrax japonica*—white flower
Honey Locust—*Gleditsia triacanthos*—green yellow flower
Siberian Iris—*Iris sibirica*—blue
Lemoine Mock Orange Hybrids—*Philadelphus lemoinei, hybrida:* Avalanche, Belle Etoile, Bonje, Boule d'Argent, Dame Blanche, Mont Blanc, etc.—double white flowers

* Raceme: A cluster of stalked flowers on a long axis

June 1-10

Glossy Buckthorn–*Rhamnus frangula*–whitish flowers
Laurel Willow–*Salix pentrandra*–catkins
American Holly–*Ilex opaca*–small white flower
Five-leaf Aralia–*Acanthopanax sieboldianus*–greenish flower
False Indigo–*Amorpha fruticosa*–violet flower
Cathay Japanese Rose–*Rosa multiflora* var. *cathayensis*–pink clusters
Climbing Rose–*Rosa Dr. W. Van Fleet*–double pale pink flower
Virginia Rose–*Rosa virginiana*–pink flower
Scotch Heather–*Calluna vulgaris* var. *rubra*–red flower
Big Scentless Mock Orange–*Philadelphus grandiflorus*–white flower
Inkberry–*Ilex glabra*–white flower
Cross-leaf Heath–*Erica tetralix*–large bright pink flower
American Yellowwood–*Cladrastis lutea*–white flower
Washington Hawthorn–*Crataegus phaenopyrum*–white flower
Amur Privet–*Ligustrum amurense*–white flower

June 10-20

Japanese Tree Lilac–*Syringa japonica*–creamy white flower
American Elder–*Sambucus canadensis*–white flower
Halls Japanese Honeysuckle–*Lonicera japonica* var. *halliana*–white flower turning yellow
Chinese Wolfberry–*Lycium chinense*–purple flower
Tatarian Honeysuckle–*Lonicera tatarica*–red fruit
Fragrant Sumac–*Rhus aromatica*–red fruit
Tree of Heaven Ailanthus–*Ailanthus altissima*–greenish panicles
Southern Catalpa–*Catalpa bignonioides*–white panicles * dotted yellow and purple
Common Winterberry–*Ilex verticillata*–white flower
California Privet–*Ligustrum ovalifolium*–white flower
Shadblow Serviceberry–*Amelanchier canadensis*–dark purplish blue
White Mulberry–*Morus alba*–white fruit
Wichura Rose–*Rosa wichuriana*–double pink clusters
Adam's Needle Yucca–*Yucca filamentosa*–creamy white flower
European Linden–*Tilia europaea*–cream flower

* Panicle: A long, loose, branching flower cluster

June 20-30

Red Mulberry—*Morus rubra*—dark red fruit
Japanese Holly—*Ilex crenata*—yellow flower
Small-leaf Japanese Holly—*Ilex crenata* var. *microphylla*—yellow flower
Convex-leaf Japanese Holly—*Ilex crenata* var. *convexa*—yellow flower
Rosebay Rhododendron—*Rhododendron maximum*—varieties in pink flowers
American Linden or American Basswood—*Tilia americana*—creamy flower
Silver Linden—*Tilia tomentosa*—creamy flower
Small-leaf European Linden—*Tilia cordata*—creamy flower

July 1-10

Japanese Snowball—*Viburnum plicatum* var. *tomentosum*—white flower, brilliant red fruit

July 10-20

Japanese Andromeda—*Pieris japonica*—racemes of yellow flower buds for next spring
Southern Catalpa—*Catalpa bignonioides*—long green fruit pods
Father Hugo Rose—*Rosa hugonis*—bright red fruit
Japanese Snowbell—*Styrax japonica*—white fruit

July 20-31

Scotch Heather—*Calluna vulgaris* var. *rosea*—pink flower
Japanese Creeper or Boston Ivy—*Parthenocissus tricuspidata*—small greenish yellow flowers
Veitch's Japanese Creeper—*Parthenocissus tricuspidata* var. *veitchi*—small greenish yellow flowers
Flame Leaf Sumac—*Rhus copallina*—white flower
Cornelian Cherry—*Cornus mas*—bright red fruit
Arrowwood—*Viburnum dentatum*—black fruit
Black Cherry—*Prunus serotina*—purplish black fruit
Ironwood, Blue Beech or American Hornbeam—*Carpinus caroliniana*—green hoplike fruit
Japanese Yew—*Taxus cuspidata*—red fruit

August 1-10

European Mountain Ash—*Sorbus aucuparia*—orange fruit
Siebold's Viburnum—*Viburnum sieboldi*—red fruit, turning black
Hercules Club or Devil's Walking Stick—*Aralia spinosa*—large creamy white flowers
Kansas Hawthorn—*Crataegus coccinioides*—large scarlet fruit
Elderberry—*Sambucus racemosa*—black-purple fruit

August 10-20

Chrysanthemum—double reddish orange flower
Spring Heath—*Erica carnea*—yellowish flower buds for next spring
Pagoda Tree—*Sophora japonica*—creamy panicles
Blood Twig Dogwood—*Cornus sanguinea*—black purple fruit
Aaron's Beard—*Hypericum calycinum*—yellow flower

August 20-31

Maple-Leaf Viburnum—*Viburnum acerifolium*—black fruit
Jetbead—*Rhodotypos scandens*—black fruit
Sassafras—*Sassafras albidum*—blue fruit
Empress Tree—*Paulownia tomentosa*—next spring's flower buds conspicuous
Rock Cotoneaster—*Cotoneaster horizontalis*—scarlet fruit
Chinese Wolfberry—*Lycium chinense*—red fruit, still flowering
Common Hackberry—*Celtis occidentalis*—black red fruit
Japanese Rose—*Rosa multiflora*—clusters of small red fruit

September 1-10

Spicebush—*Lindera benzoin*—red fruit
Flowering Dogwood—*Cornus florida*—red fruit
Scarlet Firethorn—*Pyracantha coccinea*—orange red fruit
English Hawthorn—*Crataegus oxyacantha*—bright red applelike fruit
Siberian Crab Apple—*Malus baccata*—small bright red fruit
Halls Crab Apple (Parkman)—*Malus halliana* var. *parkmani*—pea-size, dark reddish fruit

September 10-20

Laland Firethorn—*Pyracantha coccinea* var. *lalandi*—bright orange fruit

Carmine Crab Apple—*Malus atrosanguinea*—small hard red fruit

Japanese Flowering Crab Apple—*Malus floribunda*—small yellow fruit

Red Chokeberry—*Aronia arbutifolia*—red fruit

Japanese Holly—*Ilex crenata*—black fruit

Common Winterberry—*Ilex verticillata*—bright red fruit

Cockspur Thorn—*Crataegus crus-galli*—red fruit

Lily of the Valley—*Convallaria majalis*—red fruit

Japanese Creeper or Boston Ivy—*Parthenocissus tricuspidata*—blue-black fruit, foliage turns red

September 20-30

Convex-leaf Japanese Holly—*Ilex crenata* var. *convexa*—black fruit

Small-leaf Japanese Holly—*Ilex crenata* var. *microphylla*—black fruit

English Ivy—*Hedera helix*—black fruit

Spreading Cotoneaster—*Cotoneaster divaricata*—bright dark red fruit

Ground Cotoneaster—*Cotoneaster horizontalis* var. *perpusilla*—small dark red fruit

Mockernut Hickory—*Carya tomentosa*—light brown nut

California Privet—*Ligustrum ovalifolium*—black fruit

Winged Euonymus or Spindletree—*Euonymus alatus*—small red fruit

Flowering Dogwood—*Cornus florida*—bright red, purple foliage

Staghorn Sumac—*Rhus typhina*—bright red, purple foliage

Witch Hazel—*Hamamelis*—yellow flowers

Common Flowering Quince—*Chaenomeles lagenaria*—yellow-green fruit

Nannyberry—*Viburnum lentago*—blue black fruit

Sweetbay Magnolia—*Magnolia virginiana*—bright red fruit

Inkberry—*Ilex glabra*—black fruit

Common Privet—*Ligustrum vulgare*—black fruit

Washington Hawthorn—*Crataegus phaenopyrum*—small scarlet fruit in clusters

American Hornbeam—*Carpinus caroliniana*—green hoplike fruit turning brown

APPENDIX D

BIRDS OF CENTRAL PARK

Migratory and Others

Approximate date of arrival noted with the emphasis on the spring migration. Only birds frequently seen on the return flight are listed in the fall months.

Late February—Early March

Robin (summer resident)
Red-winged Blackbird
Common Grackle
American Woodcock

Early March

Yellow-shafted Flicker
Song Sparrow (also winter resident)

Mid-March

Brown-headed Cowbird
Pied-billed Grebe
Belted Kingfisher
Eastern Phoebe
Eastern Bluebird
Black-crowned Night Heron

Late March

Canada Goose (overhead)
Winter Wren
Hermit Thrush
Golden-crowned Kinglet
Eastern Meadowlark
American Goldfinch
Savannah Sparrow
Field Sparrow

Early April

White-throated Sparrow (also winter visitant)
Chipping Sparrow
Swamp Sparrow
Common Loon
American Bittern
Laughing Gull
Yellow-bellied Sapsucker
Brown Creeper
Rufous-sided Towhee
Tree Swallow
Ruby-crowned Kinglet
Pine Warbler
Palm Warbler

Mid-April

Green Heron
Chimney Swift (present in summer)
Barn Swallow
Brown Thrasher
Blue-gray Gnat Catcher
Myrtle Warbler
Louisiana Water Thrush

Late April

Northern Water Thrush
Solitary Vireo
House Wren
Spotted Sandpiper
Prairie Warbler
Black-throated Green Warbler
Yellow Warbler
Parula Warbler
Worm-eating Warbler
Black-and-white Warbler

Early May

Eastern Kingbird
Catbird
Least Flycatcher
Great Crested Flycatcher
Red-breasted Nuthatch
Wood Thrush
Veery
American Redstart
Ovenbird
Rose-breasted Grosbeak
Baltimore Oriole
Yellow-throated Vireo
Scarlet Tanager
Blue-winged Warbler
Chestnut-sided Warbler
Nashville Warbler
Black-throated Blue Warbler
Yellowthroat

Mid-May

Lincoln's Sparrow
White-crowned Sparrow
Gray-cheeked Thrush
Swainson's Thrush
Eastern Wood Peewee
Red-eyed Vireo (frequent in summer)
Indigo Bunting
Blackburnian Warbler
Canada Warbler
Wilson's Warbler
Blackpoll Warbler
Bay-breasted Warbler
Magnolia Warbler

Late May

Mourning Warbler

September

White-breasted Nuthatch
Black-capped Chickadee (also winter visitant)
Sharp-shinned Hawk
Red-shouldered Hawk
Broad-winged Hawk
Purple Finch

October

Hairy Woodpecker (also winter visitant)

November

Long-eared Owl
Saw-whet Owl

Winter Visitants

Black Duck
American Widgeon
Canvasback
Greater Scaup
Lesser Scaup
Ruddy Duck
Green-winged Teal
Common Merganser
Iceland Gull
Great Black-backed Gull
Herring Gull (also summer visitant)
Ring-billed Gull (immatures, summer visitants)
Slate-colored Junco
Tree Sparrow

All Year Transient

Blue Jay

Permanent Resident

Sparrow Hawk
Mallard (feral)
Downy Woodpecker
Starling
House Sparrow
Cardinal
Screech Owl
The Pigeon

Adapted from "The Birds of Central and Prospect Parks" by Geoffrey Carleton, *Proceedings of the Linnaean Society of New York*, December, 1958, "Birds Around New York City" by Alan D. Cruickshank, American Museum of Natural History, Popular Publications Department, and *Birds of the New York Area* by John Bull, Harper & Row, 1964.

APPENDIX E

Monuments, Tablets and Plaques (the dates shown are the dates of installation) in Central Park

Compiled by Walter Beretta, Curator of Monuments

Object	*Location*	*Description of Work*
Alice in Wonderland 1959 by José de Creeft, sculptor Hideo Sasaki, architect	Conservatory Water	Bronze group on granite esplanade
Andersen, Hans Christian 1956 by Georg Lober, sc. Otto F. Langmann, arch.	Conservatory Water	Bronze seated portrait figure on granite
Balto 1925 by Frederick G. R. Roth	At 66th Street parallel, just east of Bridge	Bronze portrait with slate tablet on natural rock
Bandstand 1923 by William G. Tachau	At north end of Mall	Limestone band shell
Bear Dancing 1937 by Frederick G. R. Roth	Zoo	Bronze
Beethoven, Ludwig van 1884 by Henry Baerer	Northwest of Mall	Bronze portrait bust and figure on granite pedestal

Object	*Location*	*Description of Work*
Bethesda Fountain 1873 by Emma Stebbins	On the Terrace at 72nd Street	Bronze sculpture on granite base and bluestone basin
Bethesda Fountain and Terrace Tablet 1965, New York Community Trust	On west wall of East Stairway	Bronze tablet
Blockhouse, War of 1812 Tablet 1905, John Williams & Co.	Just south of 110th Street at Seventh Avenue	Bronze tablet on granite block
Bolívar, Simón 1921 by Sally James Farnham	59th Street and Sixth Avenue	Bronze equestrian on granite pedestal
Brisbane, Arthur 1939 by Richard Barth, sc. Shreve, Lamb and Harmon, archs.	On Fifth Avenue at 101st Street	Relief portrait medallion forming part of granite stele
Burnett, Frances Hodgson 1936 by Bessie Potter Vonnoh	Conservatory Garden	Fountain with bronze statuette in granite basin
Burns, Robert 1880 by Sir John Steell	At south end of Mall	Bronze portrait figure on granite base
Central Park Fountain 1890 by Olin Levi Warner, arch.	East Drive at 78th Street	Granite fountain
Chidwick, Rt. Rev. Msgr. John P. 1935 by Charles Keck	Rear of Maine Monument, 59th St.	2 bronze plaques affixed to monument
City Employees' Monument, World War I, 1926 by Georg Lober, sc. Otto F. Langmann, arch.	At north end of Mall on west	Granite flagpole base with bronze appliqués

Object	*Location*	*Description of Work*
Columbus, Christopher 1894 by Jeronimo Suñol, sc. Napoleon Le Brun, arch.	South end of Mall	Bronze portrait statue on granite base
Delacorte Musical Clock 1965 by Andrea Spadini, sc. Edward C. Embury, arch.	Zoo	Animated bronze animal figures in architectural setting
Draper, Daniel 1936 by Anton Brandts Subiesky	Belvedere	Portrait plaque on tower wall
Drew, S. Rankin 1928	Mall	Bronze table on cast stone plinth
Eagles and Prey 1863 by Christian Fratin	Mall	Bronze group on granite pedestal
Eight Eagles 1941	Zoo	Free-standing granite eagles
Falconer 1872 by George Simonds	South of 72nd Cross Drive, south of west part of the Lake	Heroic bronze figure on granite pedestal
Friedsam, Michael 1951	Carousel	Bronze tablet on wall
Goat, Dancing 1937 by Frederick G. R. Roth	Zoo	Bronze
Green, Andrew Haswell 1928 by John V. and M. V. Van Pelt, archs.	East of East Drive at 104th Street	Marble bench with incised inscription
Halleck, Fitz-Greene 1877 by James Wilson Alexander MacDonald	South end of Mall	Bronze portrait statue on granite pedestal

Object	*Location*	*Description of Work*
Hamilton, Alexander 1880 by Carl Conrads	East Drive at 83rd Street	Granite portrait on pedestal
Herbert, Victor 1927 by Edmond T. Quinn	North end of Mall	Bronze bust on polished granite base with bronze lettering
Humboldt, Friedrich Heinrich Alexander von 1869 by Gustav Blaeser	East Drive at 59th Street	Bronze portrait bust on granite pedestal
Hunt, Richard Morris Memorial 1898 by Daniel Chester French, sc. Bruce Price, arch.	Fifth Avenue between 70th and 71st streets	Bronze portrait bust, center; bronze statue representing painting, south; bronze statue representing architecture, north
Hutchins, Waldo 1932 by Eric Gugler	Just north of East 72nd St. entrance	Granite bench with sundial
Indian Hunter 1869 by John Quincy Adams Ward	South end of Mall to the west	Bronze on polished granite pedestal
Jagiello, King Wladyslaw 1946 by Stanislaw K. Ostrowski, sc. Aymar Embury II, arch.	South of Great Lawn to east of Belvedere Lake	Bronze equestrian on polished granite base
Kaye, Murray P., Tablet World War II 1953	East Drive at 72nd Street	Bronze tablet on granite plinth
Kerbs, Alice Hochstader 1954	76th Street and Fifth Avenue on park wall	Bronze tablet
Kerbs, Jeanne E. 1954	Kerbs Memorial Model Boathouse	Bronze tablet on wall

Object	*Location*	*Description of Work*
Lehman Zoo Gate 1961 by Paul Manship, sc. Aymar Embury II and Edward C. Embury, archs.	Children's Zoo	Bronze gate with granite gate posts
Levy Gates 1958 by Walter Beretta, sc. John Wilson, arch.	Levy Playground near Fifth Avenue at 80th Street	Ornamental bronze gates
Loeb, Sophie Irene 1936 by Frederick G. R. Roth	Heckscher Playground	Sculptured granite drinking fountain
Maine Monument 1913 by Attilio Piccirilli, sc. H. Van Buren Magonigle, arch.	Columbus Circle	Heroic marble pylon surmounted by bronze quadriga with marble figures, fountains, gatehouses and seats
Marines of 4th Brigade Tablet, World War I 1935, Fisk Iron Works	Mall, west of Band Shell	Bronze tablet on tree guard
Marti, José Julian 1965 by Anna Hyatt Huntington, sc. Clarke and Rapuano, archs.	59th Street and Sixth Avenue	Bronze equestrian on granite pedestal
Martin, Edith 1942 by Oronzio Maldarelli	Zoo	Marble bird bath
Mazzini, Giuseppe 1878 by Giovanni Turini, sc. F. Matriati, arch.	West Drive at 62nd Street	Bronze bust on granite pedestal
McGown's Pass Cannon or Fort Clinton Cannon 1905	Overlooking Harlem Meer at 106th Street	Cannon and mortar on granite pedestal with bronze tablet

Object	*Location*	*Description of Work*
Memorial Grove, 307th Infantry 1925	East of Mall and southeast of Pergola	Bronze tablet on natural boulder and 25 bronze tablets on limestone plinths
Mitchel, John Purroy 1928 by Adolph A. Weinman, sc. Thomas Hastings and Donn Barber, archs.	90th Street on east side of Reservoir	Granite stele with gilt bronze bust, urns and stairs
Moore, Thomas 1879 by Dennis B. Sheahan	East Drive at 60th Street	Bronze bust on pedestal
Morse, Samuel Finley Breese 1871 by Byron M. Pickett	North end of Mall	Bronze portrait figure on granite pedestal
Mother Goose 1938 by Frederick G. R. Roth and Walter Beretta	Rumsey Playground	Granite group
Navy Terrace Tablet, World War II 1947	The Terrace	Bronze tablet and granite plinth in floor
Obelisk 1881	East Drive at 81st Street	Egyptian obelisk of granite resting on bronze crabs and limestone base
Osborn (William Church) Gate 1953 by Paul Manship	84th Street near Fifth Avenue	Bronze gate with granite gateposts
Park Employees' Monument 1946 by Walter Beretta	West of Mall	Bronze tablet on natural boulder
Pilgrim 1885 by John Quincy Adams Ward	East Drive at 72nd Street	Bronze statue on granite pedestal

Object	*Location*	*Description of Work*
Poth, Annie E. 1935	Southeast of Mall	Bronze tablet on granite plinth
Rumsey, Mary Harriman 1937	Rumsey Playground	Bronze tablet on wall
San Martín, José de 1951 by Luis J. Davnas	59th Street and Sixth Avenue	Bronze equestrian on granite pedestal
Schiller, Johann Christoph Friedrich von 1859 by C. L. Richter	Mall	Bronze portrait bust on granite pedestal
Scott, Richard Saunders 1947	Conservatory Water	Tablet on marble plinth
Scott, Sir Walter 1871 by Sir John Steell	South end of Mall	Bronze portrait statue on granite pedestal
Seventh Regiment Civil War Monument 1870 by John Quincy Adams Ward	West Drive at 67th Street	Bronze figure on granite pedestal
Seventh Regiment, 107th Infantry World War I Monument 1927 by Karl Morningstar Illava, sc. Rogers & Haneman, archs.	On Fifth Avenue, opposite 67th Street	Bronze group on granite base
Seventy-Seventh Division, Machine Gun Co. 307th Infantry	West of Obelisk	Bronze tablet on limestone plinth
Shakespeare, William 1864 by John Quincy Adams Ward	South end of Mall	Bronze portrait statue on granite pedestal
Shakespeare, William 1947 by Walter Beretta	Shakespeare Garden	Marble portrait bust on marble pedestal

Object	*Location*	*Description of Work*
Sherman, William Tecumseh 1903 by Augustus St.-Gaudens, sc. Charles Follen McKim, arch.	Fifth Avenue at 59th Street	Bronze equestrian group on granite base with bronze lettering and wreaths
Sims, Dr. James Marion 1894 by Ferdinand von Miller, sc. Aymar Embury II, arch.	On Fifth Avenue opposite 103rd Street	Bronze portrait statue on granite pedestal
Snow Babies 1938 by Victor Frisch	Rumsey Playground	Two cast stone figures on brick pylons
Stead, William Thomas 1920 by Sir George Frampton, sc. Carrère and Hastings, archs.	Fifth Avenue and 91st Street	Bronze portrait plaque in limestone
Still Hunt 1907 by Edward Kemeys	East Drive at 76th Street	Bronze on natural rock outcropping
Stover, Charles B. 1936 by Monuments Division, Dept. of Parks	Shakespeare Garden	Granite bench with incised inscription
Sundial 1945 by Walter Beretta	Shakespeare Garden	Bronze dial on cast stone pedestal
Szold, Henrietta 1935	West Drive opposite 83rd Street	Bronze tablet on limestone plinth
Thorvaldsen, Albert Bertel 1894 self-portrait	At 96th Street entrance near Fifth Avenue	Bronze portrait statue on pedestal with bronze lettering and medallions
Tigress and Cubs 1867 by Auguste Cain	Zoo	Bronze animal group on granite plinth

Object	*Location*	*Description of Work*
Untermeyer Fountain 1947 by Walter Schott	Conservatory Garden	Bronze group in circular pool
Vanderbilt Gate 1894 by George B. Post, arch. made by Bergrotte & Bauviller of Paris	Conservatory Garden, Fifth Avenue at 105th Street	Wrought iron gates with bronze tablet
Webster, Daniel 1876 by Thomas Ball, sc. Batterson and Canfield, archs.	72nd Street Cross Drive, at West Drive	Bronze portrait statue on granite pedestal
Wolbast, Bessie B. 1940	Mall west of Band Shell	Bronze tablet on granite plinth
Wollman, Jonas and Betty 1950	Wollman Memorial Skating Rink	Bronze tablet on wall of skate house
Young, Arthur 1949	Northwest of Hamilton statue	Bronze tablet on granite plinth

APPENDIX F

Central Park Statistics

Total acreage:	840.010 acres
total water:	150.339
total land:	689.761
Water acreage	
Reservoir:	106.601 acres
Lake:	21.836
Pool, Loch and Meer:	15.056
Belvedere Lake:	2.867
Conservatory Water:	1.818
Pond	2.161

Land acreage

North Meadow:	28.63	acres
Sheep Meadow:	12.00	
Great Lawn:	15.240	
Mall:	2.10	
19 Marginal Playgrounds:	9.124	
Heckscher Playground:	17.00	
Pedestrian Paths:	58	miles
Reservoir Path:	1.58	
Great Lawn Path:	.55	
Bridle Path	4.5	miles
Drives	6.5	miles

APPENDIX G

Acreage of Major Urban Parks of the World

Please note that not all the parks listed consist of landscaped grounds. Some, such as Jamaica Bay Park in Queens, New York, are simply large publicly owned areas designated as natural preserves.

	Size
UNITED STATES	
New York City (by Boroughs)	
Manhattan	
*Central Park	840 acres
*Morningside Park	31
*Riverside Park	266
Brooklyn	
Marine Park	1,821
*Prospect Park	526

* Designed by Frederick Law Olmsted and Calvert Vaux, or Olmsted alone.

	Size	
Bronx		
Pelham Bay Park	2,117	
Van Cortlandt	1,146	
Queens		
Alley Park	549	
Flushing Meadow Park	1,257	
Forest Park	538	
Jamaica Bay Park	9,151	(land 2,868, water 6,283)
Richmond		
Fresh Kills Park	807	
Great Kills Park	1,246	
Philadelphia		
*Fairmount Park	3,845	
Baltimore		
Druid Hill Park	675	
Herring Run Park	572	
Washington		
Rock Creek Park	1,800	
Pittsburgh		
Riverview Park	350	
Schenley Park	422	
Cleveland		
Rockefeller Park	273	
Washington Park	1,212	
Detroit		
†Belle Isle Park	985	
St. Louis		
Forest Park	1,380	

* Generally accepted as the largest park in the United States, in the strict sense of the term.

† Designed by Frederick Law Olmsted and Calvert Vaux or Olmsted alone.

	Size
Chicago	
Grant Park	303
Humboldt Park	207
*Jackson Park	543
Lincoln Park	1,185
San Francisco	
Golden Gate Park	1,107
Oakland	
East Bay Regional Parks (5)	8,200
Los Angeles	
Elysian Park	600
Griffith Park	3,761
San Diego	
Balboa Park	1,400
EUROPE	
Austria	
Vienna	
The Prater	4,270
Belgium	
Brussels	
Bois de la Cambre	272
Forêt de Soignes	9,884
Parc de Tervueren	578
Denmark	
Copenhagen	
Tivoli Gardens	23

* Designed by Frederick Law Olmsted and Calvert Vaux, or Olmsted alone.

England	
London	
Bushy Park	1,099
Hampstead Heath	790
Hyde Park	360
Kensington Gardens	275
Regent's Park (with Primrose Hill)	472
Richmond Park	2,470
France	
Paris	
Bois de Boulogne	2,155
Bois de Vincennes	2,311
Parc de St. Cloud	968
Palace of Versailles	
Gardens only	247
Germany	
Berlin	
Grunewald	4,300
Tiergarten	640 approx.
Ireland	
Dublin	
Phoenix Park	1,750
Italy	
Rome	
Villa Borghese	1,700
Florence	
Cascine	2¼ miles of frontage on the Arno

	Size
Russia	
Leningrad	
Kirov Central Park of Culture and Rest	250 approx.
Moscow	
Dzerzhinsky Recreation Park and Main Botanical Garden of the U.S.S.R. Academy of Sciences	990
Spain	
Madrid	
Casa del Campo	4,317
El Retiro	353

APPENDIX H

Further Reading

C. Frank Brockman, *Trees of North America.* (Golden Press, N.Y., 1968). A handy paperback in the Golden Field Guide series.

John Bull, *Birds of the New York Area.* (Harper & Row, New York, 1964). The best available book on birds in and around the city.

Clarence Cook, *A Description of the New York Central Park.* (Benjamin Blom, Inc., New York, 1972). Published originally in 1869, it is the best of the early guides to the park.

Andrew Jackson Downing, *A Treatise on the Theory and Practice of Landscape Gardening.* (Funk & Wagnalls, N.Y., 1967). The most famous book on the picturesque landscape by an American in a reprint edition.

Ralph Dutton, *The English Garden.* (B. T. Batsford, London, 1958). An excellent short history of the subject.

James Thomas Flexner, *The Pocket History of American Painting.* (Washington Square Press, New York, 1962). For the chapter on the Hudson River School of painting.

Ernest de Ganay, *Les Jardins de France.* (Librairie Larousse, Paris, 1949). The history of French gardening, to contrast with that of the English. A model of its kind in scholarship and style.

Marie Louis Gothein, *A History of Garden Art.* (E. P. Dutton, New York, 1928). 2 vols. The definitive history of world gardening. Out of print.

M. M. Graff, *Tree Trails in Central Park.* (Greensward Foundation, New York, 1970). Essential for anyone who wants to know about the park's trees. Obtainable from museum and other bookshops.

Arthur Harmount Graves. *Illustrated Guide to Trees and Shrubs.* (Harper & Brothers, New York, 1956). A handy guide to identify plants, with a winter key.

Alma C. Guillet. *Make Friends of Trees and Shrubs: The People's Park.* (Doubleday, New York, 1962). Description of trees to be found in Central Park.

William H. Harlow, *Trees of the Eastern and Central United States and Canada.* (Dover, New York, 1942). A paperback guide.

Christopher Hussey, *The Picturesque.* (Frank Cass, London, 1967). A very entertaining history of the Picturesque and its part in transforming the English landscape by an editor of *Country Life.*

Frederick Law Olmsted, *Cityscape and Landscape: Frederick Law Olmsted's Plans for a Greater New York.* Albert Fein, editor. (Cornell University Press, Ithaca, 1967). A collection of Olmsted's writings accompanied by an introductory essay and notes.

Frederick Law Olmsted, Jr., and Theodora Kimball, editors, *Frederick Law Olmsted, Landscape Architect 1822–1903.* (Benjamin Blom, Inc., New York, 1970). Key source of the history of Central Park.

Roger Tory Peterson, *A Field Guide to the Birds, Giving Field Marks of All Species Found East of the Rockies.* (Houghton Mifflin, Boston, 1947). The bird watcher's handbook.

Roger Tory Peterson and Margaret McKenny, *A Field Guide to Wild Flowers.* (Houghton Mifflin, Boston, 1968). The best wildflower guide available.

Christopher J. Schuberth, *The Geology of New York City and Environs.* (The Natural History Press, Garden City, N.Y., 1968). An illustrated guide to the city's geology with very useful material on the rock outcrops of Central Park.

Christopher Tunnard, *The City of Man.* (Charles Scribner's Sons, New York, 1953). See the chapter, "The Romantic Mood," on the landscaping fever of pre-Civil War years.

Christopher Tunnard and Henry Hope Reed, *American Skyline.* (New American Library, New York, 1956). A Mentor paperback that tells how changing fashions in landscape and garden have influenced the shape of the American city.